How to Start and Successfully Operate a Charter School

An In-Depth Guide Detailing How to Start
And Operate A Successful Charter School

Dr. John von Rohr

Order this book online at www.trafford.com
or email orders@trafford.com

Most Trafford titles are also available at major online book retailers.

Co-Author of the "Time Management Resource Guide," printed by the U.S. Govt Printing
Office, West Point, NY and numerous articles in professional journals

Print information available on the last page.

ISBN: 978-1-4907-5125-2 (sc)

Library of Congress Control Number: 2014920430

Trafford rev. 02/25/2016

www.trafford.com
North America & international
toll-free: 1 888 232 4444 (USA & Canada)
fax: 812 355 4082

TABLE OF CONTENTS

Appendices

DEDICATION

To my loving mother, Maxine (1921-2008), who taught me to be resilient and my father, Duane (1922-1995) who undoubtedly passed onto me, unconsciously, his life-long nature of paying attention to detail.

ACKNOWLEDGEMENTS

It would not have been possible to ever complete this book without the many people who provided technical information to me, in particular about charter school construction and renovation: Jim Carson at Smithson Construction, Steve Earnhardt at Vanguard Modular, Patrick Munchmore at Williams-Scotsman, and Torrey Rush at Integrity Real Estate Investors. In the field of school finance, I am indebted to Bill Moser at Kelley-Moser Consulting in Lexington, SC, Dorothy Leonard in Rocky Mount, NC and Fran Shelton in Greensboro, NC. Joel Medley and Dr. Wayne Brazell, Director of Charter Schools in North Carolina and Superintendent of the South Carolina Public Charter School District, respectively, deserve recognition for their support of this writing effort, along with my "personal support team" consisting of Dr. Patricia Schreiber, educational consultant in Kernersville, North Carolina and Ms. Caroline Upchurch, former mentee, now a successful school administrator in her own right in Charlotte, North Carolina. More kudos are deserved by my South Carolina charter school colleagues, Mr. Adam Ademci at Green Charter School and Dr. Karen Wicks at Royal Live Oaks Academy, for providing me with information about building projects on their campuses. Finally, to my lovely wife, Larissa, who put up with me, hour after hour, during my absence while I completed this book. I am now able to ask her "what do you want to do today, my love?"

APPENDICES

INTRODUCTION

There is no hidden agenda in regard to my intent in writing this book; it is, quite specifically, to provide charter school boards and administrators with a user-friendly "how to guide" to start up and/or successfully operate a charter school. After almost sixteen years of experience in charter schools, I feel I am in an excellent position to offer you guidance about charter school operation. Beware! At points in the book I will offer very detailed information (e.g. Five Year and Monthly Budget at Appendices L and M), while at other times I will be writing in a first person narrative while reporting real life experiences and their impact on "surviving" in charter schools (e.g. Chapter 1). Furthermore, at times I may sound quite serious, such as when I am providing you with what might be called charter school basics; and at other junctures be quite tongue in cheek while searching for humor in what otherwise might have then been described as "charter school chaos."

It does not take a genius, and I do not claim to be one, to come to the conclusion that the great majority of charter schools fail because of poor leadership and/ or poor financial management. I will cover each of these topics at length in this book. I have no "magic wand" to wave at you from afar at my charter school here in South Carolina, only the knowledge about what will most often work or not work in charter schools. With my current school's designation as a Blue Ribbon Lighthouse School and three straight years receiving "A's" on the state report card, I have reached what I recognize to be the pinnacle of my career, because of one particular leadership dimension at my disposal, the ability to select the highest quality teachers and support staff. My many, many great staff members (this includes both instructional and administrative personnel) over the years have undoubtedly made a significant contribution toward my success as a charter school leader. To deny this would be pure arrogance.

When I started out at my first charter school in 1999 in rural North Carolina, I had no idea what I was getting myself into, but I did recognize I would be challenged. In writing this book, I have made a purposeful attempt to help both board of directors and school administrators avoid some of the frustration and pitfalls I have experienced, by either not being knowledgeable enough myself or by not knowing who to call for assistance. Something as simple as knowing what type of daily operational plans you will need, or copies of typical correspondence, can make the difference between looking for another school leadership position or finding real peace in your charter school workplace.

I do not claim that this book is the "end all" for charter school operation, but it does cover a significant amount of the territory you will need to be familiar with in order to achieve success in the unique world of charter school operation. What is the degree of difficulty you may likely experience in your efforts to obtain information crucial to getting your charter school started? The truth is; it may be daunting. For example: one of my former Assistant Principals, Caroline Upchurch, who went on to become a very successful Principal in her own right at Lake Lure Classical Academy in North Carolina, advised me that when she went to an interview for another school leadership position at an about-to-be-opened charter school, they actually asked her more questions about how to start a charter school than any about her professional qualifications for the position she was interviewing for. This has to tell you something; there are plenty of people out there who are very enthusiastic about opening charter schools (it really is an exciting proposal, isn't it?); yet they know very little about how to get a school off the ground in the first place, in particular in regard to finding a suitable location for a charter school (M.C. Upchurch, personal communication, March 12, 2014).

A review of this book will hopefully answer many of the questions you have about either starting or successfully operating a charter school, hence the title of this book. A couple of quick comments: I am not going to address the topic of writing a charter proposal. The best advice I've ever heard on this topic came from Joel Medly, current Director of Charter Schools at the North Carolina Department of Public Instruction. I asked Joel for his guidance on this issue in 2009 when several parents at my school asked me to write a proposal for a charter high school. His recommendation was incredibly simple, "review copies of successful charter applications and adapt yours to one's that have been approved" (J. Medley, personal communication, March 17, 2009). In other words, why try to reinvent the wheel when most parts of it already exist? Of course, your charter school will be unique, but after twenty years of charter applications being presented and approved, using examples from those already approved is an astute idea. Writing a charter is your first step; once you've turned in your application, the time is right to begin exploring where your school could be located if your charter is approved. The charter school movement in the United State has already proven the time is right for more schools of choice. It is my hope that this book will serve as a valuable source of information for both start-up charters and those already in operation; a resource that will lead you to a high degree of success in your personal endeavors to improve educational opportunities in this country.

If you are interested in contacting me to ask questions or personally facilitate your charter school's operation, please feel free to email me at jmvonrohr@ aol.com or call me at (864) 764-4722. I look forward to assisting you in any way possible.

Best Regards,
Dr. John von Rohr
October 2014

CHAPTER 1

Finding a Location

Part I – Rocky Mount Charter School (RMCS) -Renovation of Facilities

Finding a location in which to start up or successfully operate a charter school poses what will very likely be your biggest and most problematic issue to contend with. Do you build a school facility from the ground up, do you renovate a building already sitting empty, or do you imagine setting up a modular campus for either short of long-term use? I will attempt to address each of these possibilities, with the goal of helping you determine which best suits your charter school's individual needs.

Rocky Mount Charter School (later renamed Rocky Mount Preparatory School) obtained its charter in 1998 through the support of three influential community members, each of whom personally co-signed on a loan of about $800,000 to renovate an empty J.C. Penney store located in what was then known as the Tarrytown Mall in Rocky Mount, North Carolina.

The loan was initially secured through a credit union in Durham, North Carolina and Centura Bank, one of the largest in the state. It was a tremendous advantage to have the former CEO of this bank on the Board of Directors. Before the school opened and seeing a need for assistance in running the school, the board contracted with an educational management company (EMO), with the goal of helping the school with financial support and assistance in implementing curricular/educational programs at the school.

The school opened in August 1998, with three classes for each grade, kindergarten through fifth, adding a new grade (with a need for three new classrooms) each school year after that. The former J.C Penny facility consisted of a total of about 60,000 square feet. There was square footage allocated in the operational plans for the eventual build-out of the school to grade eight, to include a gym in what was once used as a warehouse by the department store.

The school opened with 600 students in kindergarten through fifth. The school had THREE Principals in the period August 1998 through March 1999, when I arrived. From what I was told my first day on the job in March 1999, the first Principal contracted with quit within two weeks, noting the job was too much for them; the second was let out of their contract when it was determined their spouse thought the job too time consuming; while the third was identified as an "Interim Principal," supplied by the management company, with the intent to only serve in the position until Rocky Mount Charter's Board of Directors could find the next school leader, who happened to be yours truly. The issue of "Hiring Administrative Leaders" is covered in Chapter 6.

In August of 1999, the school began its second school year and was prepared to serve three new classes of sixth graders (our fifth graders had moved up a grade). A new playground was complete (constructed by parents and staff members) and the former warehouse was now operational as a gym. As part of the original charter, we used twelve school-owned busses to transport our mostly urban student population to and from school each day. I will provide more information on bus cost in a later chapter.

Only a month later, in early September, Hurricane Dennis rumbled through eastern North Carolina with torrential rains, the water not seeming to want to be absorbed into the ground, but just lying there on the surface. After a one week respite from the bad weather, Hurricane Floyd made its way into Eastern

North Carolina, wreaking havoc in its path. Rocky Mount Charter was located in a one hundred year flood plain, so no could realistically expect what would happen next.

As Hurricane Floyd passed through Rocky Mount and rain continued to fall, the city became composed of three "islands," those above water on high ground, those with moderate flooding and those underwater. It was a sad sight indeed when I was able to travel to the school and measured the water line, which was 5'2" above ground level, totally destroying what was an $800,000 investment in this charter school.

While the school was much more than a "business" to the school's Board of Directors, their intent was to go on, no matter what. I was personally advised by our board chair (R. Mauldin, personal communication, October 1999) that the EMO did not believe the school would ever be financially solvent after the flood; therefore they would willingly negate their contract with the school. It was determined that the school had flood insurance and these funds were split equally between the two parties. The policy was around $500,000, so although some money was recovered it was not enough to make up for the loss of the school facility, only enough to keep the school operating, somewhere.

Part II –RMCS Moves in Churches

We were out of school for only two weeks, after which time, with assistance from our influential Board of Directors, we moved into three church sites in Rocky Mount; three hundred students located at two different churches in the downtown area and one hundred students at a third church, located some five miles away from the downtown area. This was initially perceived as a logistical "nightmare," but a staff composed of highly intelligent, motivated and dedicated staff kept the school operating under some very trying conditions. As Principal, I was located at one downtown church, while my Curriculum Director supervised student activity at the second downtown location. A Senior/Lead Teacher was in charge of the K-1 students at the school site five miles away. I paid twice-weekly visits to the "remote site" and was in daily contact with the Senior/Lead Teacher.

The "little kids" (grades K-1) were situated at the church located five miles away due to the fact the facility was all on ground level and there are usually local fire codes that prohibit children kindergarten to second grade students from being above the first floor in an educational setting.

The best part of this relocation was that we kept the school operational, with 97% of our original student body intact at the three churches. Due to the graciousness of the church leaders we imposed on, we paid a very small fee for monthly rent. Our school's plight received national attention and donations were received from school children and other benefactors from all over the United States. I still keep a box of school supplies sent to me as Principal after this disaster, as a reminder of how generous "strangers" can be. Many people, from both other charter and traditional public schools, saw us for what we really were, a public school that had suffered an immeasurable blow to its ability to successfully educate students.

Do you have questions about locating a charter school in a church setting? I hope so, and now I will attempt to point out some important questions you need to ask yourself:

What will your monthly rent be?

Is the monthly rent reasonable for the square footage you will be using?

Do you have an agreement to take down religious items (e.g. crosses, pictures of Jesus, etc.) in classrooms before you start school on Mondays and a similar agreement to return them to their original position for use by the church on the weekend?

Do all of your proposed classroom settings meet local fire code requirements?

Will the school be allowed to operate totally under your control during the school week?

Will you have appropriate office space for administrators at the location?

Will this location be separate from the location of the regular church operation (e.g. upstairs and downstairs, or separate parts of the church facility?)

Part III – RMCS Moves into Modular Classrooms

After six months in churches, we moved into about thirty double-wide modular classrooms on the far west side of town. The modulars were rented from the Williams-Scotsman offices in Durham, North Carolina. The mobile home park we moved into was new and had only about fifteen out of a total of about two hundred spaces in use. We were located at the far end of the park, in our own little parcel on the property. In addition to regular classroom space for three classes of each grade, kindergarten through sixth, we also had modular buildings for administrators (co-located in the same modular as the school's office) and storage space (for textbooks, furniture, storage, etc.). We no longer had any school furniture (all of it was "totaled" in the flood due to contamination from toxic flood water damage) so we made inquiries to the local public school district, Nash County Schools. Their local Superintendent advised us that they had closed an elementary school in the county and that we could have that furniture, for free. That "gift" was instrumental in our survival and is an example of how, in time of need, traditional public schools can be a friend and supporter of their charter school neighbors. Recommendation: Do not hesitate to establish a good relationship with the traditional public school leaders in your community. You are not "competitors" but "partners" when it comes to educating the children in your community. I would highly recommend that you take the first step in establishing a good working relationship with your local educational counterparts.

Part IV – RMCS -Building a School from the Ground Up

With a $4.6 million dollar grant (described in Chapter 18 under Grant Writing) from FEMA, architectural plans were drawn up by Smithson Construction, located in Rocky Mount, North Carolina (See Appendix A) for a 70,000 square foot school. Both school administrators and teaching staff were involved in providing a list of "needs" for the new school building and they were incorporated into the final design. After several sites were considered, our Board of Directors decided to build the new school on a thirty-two acre site on the north side of town, about five miles from the school's original location in downtown Rocky Mount. The new school was to be situated right across the street from a private four year college, North Carolina Wesleyan College.

In what seemed to be an almost improbable project, Smithson Construction, under the direction of Mr. Jim Carson, completed the entire school project in time to open our doors in August of 2001. Photographs of the completed school can be found at Appendix B. Documentation noting the period of extreme turmoil from 1999-2000 can be found at Appendix C, verifying we moved the entire school from one location to another **TWO TIMES** in one school year. The **THIRD** move of the entire school, from the mobile home park to the permanent school facility, took place in 2001. If you can find one, permanent place for your school to be located, more power to you. Unfortunately, it is not entirely unusual for a charter schools to initially locate in one place and then move to another, that is why "Finding a Location" is a critical issue for charter school founders.

Our monthly mortgage payments were initially about $18,000 per month on the $3.5 million dollar loan. At that time, our yearly revenue exceeded $3 million dollars, with 700 students and increased as our enrollment went up each year as we progressed toward our goal of having a K-12 school. We were in a much better financial position at this time, so much so that we were able to purchase all new classroom furniture for the school.

After this first year of our existence at our new school site, a 20,000 square foot high school wing was added and construction of an 18,000 square foot gym, with offices, a weight room and showers for both boys and girls followed shortly thereafter. This new construction added about $2 million to our financed debt and raised our monthly mortgage payments to about $30,000 per month (D. Leonard, personal communication, October 24, 2014). By 2003, the school's board of directors decided to better define their educational mission by changing the school's name to "Rocky Mount Preparatory School." According to Jim Carson (personal communication, February 10, 2014) the 2014 cost for building a school similar to Rocky Mount Prep in today's construction dollars would be between $12.5-15 million.

Part V – Another Example of Renovation & Rental

After leaving Rocky Mount in June of 2004, in August of that same year I assumed Principal duties at another start up charter school in central North Carolina, one which was initially located in what used to be a church. The student body numbered around three hundred. This school had also contracted with an EMO for financial assistance and curricular guidance. The church had been purchased by the EMO and had been renovated for school use, at a cost less than $100,000.00. The classrooms in this school setting were smaller than educator-desirable (a minimum of 750 square feet versus the 450 square feet in this facility), but the school ran well for the first year, after which time and EMO and Board of Directors parted ways. The church/school property consisted of about 26,000 square feet and the EMO charged us $26,000 per month in rent.

Since the EMO owned the property and the school's Board of Directors did not want to purchase it, the school had no choice but to look for another school-appropriate campus setting.

I have absolutely no doubt, as a result of my personal experience, that locating a school-appropriate site for your charter school will be the most confounding issue/obstacle presented to you when starting up, or relocating. While in the previously stated instance with the EMO a decision was made to disengage with the management company before the end of the school year, we were not able to secure a new location until well into the summer due to one thing or another, in several instances due to fire codes.

After months of looking, a parent at the school found a very large local church that had a second, separate building on its grounds. A modular classroom, newly in place, was located in the parking across from the main church building. It served as the setting for the school office, Business Manager, Principal and one kindergarten classroom. The second kindergarten class and all students in grades one to three students attended classes on the first floor (approximately 6,000 square feet), main building, in classrooms of about 500 square feet each, while the upstairs (approximately 14,000 square feet) was open space that was divided up by partitions into separate classrooms for students in grades four through eight. There was no option for putting up permanent walls; this was not allowed by the rental agreement. We were going back to the "old school days," when open classrooms were in vogue in the early 1980's. Teachers taught and students learned; it was the quality of the teachers that made up for any logistical problems we had. The message I am attempting to impart here should be clear; that all people associated with charter schools need to be flexible, flexible, flexible.

After moving school furniture and literally everything else associated with the school from one location to the other (all moving accomplished by the school staff to keep expenses down), we opened the school's second year in this new location. One unavoidable drawback was the monthly rent payment, which was expensive at about $13,000 per month for about 20,000 square feet of school space. The monthly payment put the school in a poor financial position from then on. The students were high achievers, the staff was great, but we always knew our survival depended heavily upon our ability to pay that big monthly rent payment.

Part VI – Renovation of Former School Facility

From 1939-1971 Southside Elementary School was located at 385 S. Spring Street in downtown Spartanburg, South Carolina. In 1971, the local school district built a new school facility and the school site sat abandoned until 1974, when the property was purchased by the Arts Partnership of Greater Spartanburg. From 1974 to 2007, the school served as a local arts center, eventually relocating to the newly constructed Chapman Cultural Center about a mile away. Most notably, before sale to the Spring Street Group in 2008, the Arts Partnership sold 1.45 acres of the property, located at the rear of the school, to the South Carolina Employment Commission. The Spring Street Group sold the reduced in size former Southside Elementary School to the founders of Spartanburg Charter School in 2008. The school legally changed its name to "Spartanburg Preparatory School (SPS)" on July 1, 2013.

With money from an implementation grant from the State of South Carolina, the initial founders of the school began an ambitious renovation process under the direction of a retired engineer, who provided me with information on early construction costs (T. Petoskey, personal communication, March 3, 2014). According to Petoskey, the initial expenditure for bringing the lower of two floors up to code for the 2009-2010 school year was about $70,000.00 (Phase I).

When the school opened to 231 students in August of 1999, it looked much different than when first purchased; although there were still many remnants of 1939 still in place, like the original boiler and windows, installed when "Gone with the Wind" and "The Wizard of Oz" were first shown in movie theatres throughout the United States.

In the summer of 2010, about 1/3 of the second floor was renovated (Phase II), at a cost of about $200,000, to house fifth and sixth grade students. A false wall was put up on the second floor so that visitors did not recognize the fact that there was quite a sizable amount of the school remaining to be completed. In the summer of 2011, with charter school funding almost doubled in the State of

South Carolina (but still under the national average and only half as much as our local public school district receives in per student funding) the second floor was completed at cost of about $225,000. The total square footage of the second floor was close to 20,000 square feet. The layout of this school may be viewed at Appendix D.

In the summer of 2013, all of the 1939 era windows were replaced at a cost of about $400,000, the boiler at a cost of $50,000 and the 1970's era air conditioning system in the cafeteria for close to $45,000 (C. Smith, personal communication, October 24, 2014). Where did funding for these projects come from? Along with the increased state funding, the school had won $500,000 in Kohl's Department Store contest (see Chapter 18 on Grant Writing for more details). Once the school had sufficient funding to keep the school operating, it was run very efficiently, with oversight provided by the school's Board of Directors. The board long ago decided to keep the school in a K-8 configuration. Since the school is almost "nuclear safe" due its sound structural heritage, it was always their intent to continue to renovate the school facility versus looking for a new school campus setting elsewhere. I fully concur with my board's decision to remain in our current location since it is our staff, students and their parents that serve as the foundation for our success; the building is merely the vessel into which we "pour" all the ingredients.

Other Examples of Renovating Buildings for Charter School Use

The Green Charter School opened its doors in 2013 in a 22,000 square foot building formerly occupied by a health and fitness club. Through the assistance of a real estate developer, at an initial cost of about $1.7 million dollars (monthly payments $27,500), the school served about 280 students in grades kindergarten through sixth, with two sections each grade, twenty students in 550-600 square foot classrooms. In 2014, an additional 8,000 square feet of available space in the building will be turned into classrooms. The Green Charter School will eventually serve students in grades K-12 (A. Ademci, personal communication, February 20, 2014). Green Charter School's floor plan is located at Appendix E.

It was not an easy proposition finding companies who would be upfront and honest with me about the cost of renovation, but I was fortunate to establish a good relationship with Mr. Torrey Rush, Director of Advisory Services at Integrity Real Estate Advisors in Columbia, South Carolina. Torrey was enthusiastic about providing me with information that would help charter school people make decisions about school sites and their costs. Torrey's company has built and/or renovated charter schools. The information he provided to me (T. Rush, personal communication, February 4, 2014) was not the slightest bit theoretical, which I greatly appreciated, since I found that numerous companies involved with renovating buildings for charter schools were not forthcoming. I feel compelled to provide you with reliable information for your planning purposes.

The floor plan for the two-story design Orangeburg Charter for Health Professions, a charter school located in Orangeburg, South Carolina, can be found at Appendix F. This was an existing building converted into a grade nine through twelve school campus. Two hundred eighty students with an interest in health careers now occupy this 16,000 square charter school renovation project, located on three acres. Services provided by Integrity Real Estate Advisor's include charter school site identification, contract negotiations, due diligence, design concept, development management and long-term facility management. The overall project cost was $2.8 million dollars.

Mr. Rush has also provided plans for transforming a 21,000 square foot office building into a charter school that would house three hundred forty-five students. The cost for this project, designated for planning purposes as North Main Academy, is $2.5 million dollars. The lay-out of this school is also located at Appendix F.

Modular Classrooms/School Sites

Royal Live Oaks Academy of the Arts and Sciences Charter School opened for the 2013-2014 school year in a rural area of South Carolina's "Low Country" with 450 students in grades kindergarten through eighth, with the intent of eventually becoming a K-12 school. Eleven modular double-wide units (approximately 70' by 23') were installed, along with a triple-wide administrative building (approximately 70' by 36', including offices, a reception area, an open area, bathrooms and kitchen) on a thirty-three acre site donated by a local school district. A county public school, abandoned, is still located on the grounds, with the new modular buildings on the more than adequate remaining open space (see the school's physical layout at Appendix G). The cost of the school facility included $350,000.00 for site work, and an upfront deposit of $100,000.00. The school will pay monthly payments of about $20,000.00 for the thirty-six month financing term (K. Wicks, personal communication, February 20, 2014).

On March 1, 2014, Vanguard Modular's Stephen Earnhardt (personal communication, January 28, 2014) provided me with specific information, to include costs, for a 168' by 65' modular classroom school encompassing 10,920 square feet. A floor plan for the proposed campus is also provided for your review at Appendix H, along with a "Modular Project Description," listing set-up costs. Vanguard Modular has extensive experience in building modular campus sites, which may be viewed at their website (www.vanguardmodular.com). For estimating purposes, the monthly rent on one modular unit runs about $400 per month, with a per unit set-up cost of about $6,000 (S. Earnhardt, personal communication, February 20, 2014). Note: My current charter school rents one modular classroom at a cost of $400 per month.

Williams-Scotsman, who provided Rocky Mount Charter with modular classrooms in 2000, continues to provide modular school settings on a national basis. Thanks to Patrick Munchmore (personal communication, February 21, 2014) and Tracy Cassidy (personal communication, February 21, 2014) at Williams-Scotsman, I am able to offer you photographs and floor plans for two schools; Soldier Hollow Charter School in Midway, Utah and Griffithville Elementary School in Griffithsville, West Virginia.

The Spider Hollow campus consists of over 6,000 square feet of modular classroom space with the intent of educating one hundred students in grades K-8. It is located near a former Olympic cross country ski venue. According to the documentation provided by Williams-Scotsman, they received the order to build on January 1, 2010 and completed installation of the modular setting on August 13, of the same year. Photographs of the school and floor plan may be viewed at Appendix I.

The Griffithsville Elementary School modular project consisted of eight detached modular structures and, according to the accompanying literature and photographs, about 20,077 square feet divided into nineteen classrooms. The information provided by Williams-Scotsman notes an overall start to finish time of three months versus a stick-built timeline of six to nine months for completion (Information on the Griffithsville School is attached at Appendix I).

School Construction Update – September 2014

Literally weeks before turning in the final manuscript of this book to publishers, while sitting in my office, I pondered the thought, "where do we go from here, we could just coast now if we wanted to." In other words, I could just continue to fine-tune my school by continuing to employ the best teachers available. Referred to by my former board Chairman (M. Gilley, personal communication, July 21, 2014) as having a "laser focused leadership style," I have rejected complacency and continue to be as forward thinking as circumstances permit.

As a result of writing this book, I have been obligated to reflect back to the 1999-2001 time period, when my charter school went from destruction to transiency, to "rebirth" in a built from the ground up school facility. Once again, I must determine "what's next?" The answer has come to me quite clearly; make the school even better and more attractive to potential students and their families. This has very quickly taken the form of my recommendation for new construction, turning the now open space (courtyard) into three separate classrooms of approximately 750 square feet each, demolishing the current cafeteria, building a new one in its place and adding a high school size gymnasium. The gym to be built would come close to replicating the one built in Rocky Mount, NC in 2001; it would have offices, storage space, locker rooms for home and visiting teams, a snack bar and boys and girls bathrooms in the lobby area.

The cost for this approximately 23,000 square foot project is roughly $2 million dollars (J. Carson, personal communication, September 10, 2014). With a very bright financial position at this time, we are having no problems finding financial institutions interested in assisting us with financing and, if this project comes to fruition, we would roll our current mortgage balance of about $700,000 into the $2 million for an overall debt of $2.7 million. At current mortgage rates, our monthly payment on a twenty-year fixed mortgage would be about $16,500 per month; for fifteen years, $19,500 per month (B. Mason, personal communication, September 23, 2014). My advice to our board of directors, upon approval, will be to take the twenty year term and mortgage and pay it off early. The $16,500 per month figure covers the debt for about 64,000 square feet of school facility space. This project is currently under consideration by my board of directors.

As a final note, once you have your concept mind, be sure you allow multiple designers/contractors to bid on your projects; even if your state law does not require such a process for you as a charter school. I have more advice, what I will characterize as a "strong recommendation," reference any building project. Do not automatically give the contract for a building project to a local contractor or design firm, make sure you obtain multiple bids. Please ensure the person you are going to use to construct your school does not have an "additional" personal motive for being involved in the process, e.g. he/she owns the property they want you to build on. The consequences for doing business with local "friends" can be catastrophic, to include getting a bad site for your school or, at its worst, never getting the school built. Warning: watch out, charter schools in rural areas where the "old boy system" remains in place; it is not good for your school, your students, their families or your overall financial position to automatically use local "friends" to build your charter school.

CHAPTER 2

Determining Student Population to Serve

It is entirely possible that you have already decided what grade configuration you will propose in your charter, however, I can offer you some personal advice after being actively associated with charter schools for the past sixteen years.

The bottom line is, from my own personal experience and from speaking with experienced charter school colleagues is that the K-8 configuration usually produces the best results. In particular, if you start out with grades K-5 and add one grade per year, versus starting out at K-8, I firmly believe your chances for success will be much higher.

This personal hypothesis applies not only to academics, but also behavior. As you will later read in Chapter 11 (Code of Conduct), I have not experienced any serious behavioral issues at any of the schools I have had operational control of, even with very dissimilar student populations. When students are brought up in an environment of mutual respect and kindness, they have a distinct tendency to behave that way throughout their daily interactions at school. And, in regard to how to "train" your students in how to be good citizens, I highly recommend a structured Character Education program, which 80% of the charter schools I've served at have incorporated into their curriculum.

As stated, I do believe the K-8 configuration seems to works best for several reasons, which I will now attempt to explain. When you go the K-12 route, even "growing" your students on the way up, you may find possible impediments to high overall achievement due to the number and complexity of high school end of course requirements. At Rocky Mount Prep, I began developing the high school curriculum when we only had seventh graders. What we ended up with was a great group of students who were taking some really creative high courses, designed to provide a "classical education" to ALL of our students, to include making it mandatory for all tenth graders to enroll in "Art History." At Rocky Mount Prep, we had one of only three high school programs in the entire United States to offer "Archeology" to juniors and seniors. This course was not theoretical, but hands-on and included students participating in a field dig with college students from William & Mary College in Virginia. Students who were involved in the dig that day near City Point, VA found five hundred years of history at their fingertips!

The "unwritten" story about charter schools that offer K-12 programs is there for you to examine, if you look closely and ask the right questions. At Rocky Mount Prep, to ensure that our graduation requirements were challenging enough for our highest achieving students, we offered dual enrollment college credit courses. We also initiated a somewhat less rigorous, but still challenging graduation track curriculum for our somewhat less studious students and a third track for students with learning disabilities, if their Individual Education Plan noted it. We were realists, not idealists, when we set up the high school program, realizing that our projected curriculum could be, by its very rigorous nature, too challenging for some of our lower achieving students or those with physical and/or learning disabilities. Note: The percentage of non-disabled students who went on to some form of college program after the school's first two years was 100% (G. Williamson, August 15, 2012). I propose this was an example of a K-12 curriculum that worked very efficiently for our entire student body, one that was the result of the entire staff working together for the benefit of each and every high school student.

The bare reality of going K-12 is that you are going to have much higher staff costs because high school requires a wide variety of classes being offered, in particular for electives, to include Advance Placement courses (if you are going "high end" on the curriculum). High school classes tend to have fewer students in them, which means a higher cost per classroom. Note: Don't get me wrong, I love high school students, but they are much more "needy." Don't think you can get away with not having a high school counselor for your high school students; one for the entire school will invariably not be enough. Another consideration is extracurricular activities for high school students.

You may think you have the greatest academic program in all the land, but if you don't have clubs AND high school athletics you will lose students after middle school, maybe even before that if you did not have some competitive middle sports for them. If you plan on putting on sports programs, be prepared to allocate money for coaches and facility rental; a significant amount of money if you are not very careful. My suggestion: put a line item in your budget to cover these areas. If you can initiate a really effective parent support group to keep your developing sports program going, you will be at a distinct advantage over trying to do it all on your own. And, at the high school level, you will, not too long after starting a program, have to have someone to serve as your Athletic Director, which is another payroll consideration. You can start your program by paying a physical education teacher a stipend for the additional time required, or by reducing their classroom load. When you think "coaches" you need to recognize that higher payroll costs are going to be a reality and at some point you will not be able to continue with parent volunteers. How much do you pay someone to coach your students? For the 2014-2015 school year, we are past the "volunteer coach stage" and will be paying our head coaches $1,000.00 per season, while Assistant coaches will receive $750.00.

When your 9th to 12th grade curriculum is too tough and/or unrealistic for all, you will very likely experience what I describe the "funnel effect" at K-12 charter schools: you will most likely have a large number of elementary students, fewer students in the middle school and a much smaller number of students in the high school. I have personally spoken to numerous Principals of K-12 charter high schools and they readily admit the "funnel effect" is the reality. Why does this occur? The answer is quite simple; when you are promoting a curriculum with "classical education" requirements for your high school students, requiring

Algebra I, Algebra II and two years of Latin, you will very likely find that the "average high school" student is not up to the challenge.

I once wondered how some K-12 charter schools with particularly tough curriculums "beat" their stated mandated reporting of dropout rates. The answer is once again simple; they noted the students transferred to another high school, thus negating the need to report these students as "drop-outs." We never played this "game" during my time at Rocky Mount Prep. In the 2001-2004 time frame, we offered a curriculum that was both tough and inclusive enough to suit all of our students.

Another thing to watch out for is trying to offer "too much, too soon." I strongly recommend your find your charter school's academic "niche" and work to improve on it, making it the very best it can be. In particular, start-up charter schools that advertise not only a challenging curriculum, but also sports, ballet, drama, chorus and almost every possible elective for their students need to take a hard look, wake up and think about all the costs they are going to incur. I will claim seniority as a charter school leader on this topic and propose that offering "too much" can be as bad not offering enough.

While attending an educator's conference at North Carolina State University a few years ago, their admission's office "experts" put forth the proposal that a student's Algebra I grade is the most credible predictor of success in college (graduation). If you agree with this hypothesis; you are most likely a college graduate.

Your teaching staff is going to make the biggest difference when it comes to success or something short of it. I have always supported the proposition that the senior instructional leader mimics the leadership model noted by former New York Yankee slugger Reggie Jackson in that you are, as Principal, "the straw that stirs the drink" (http://en.wiksipedia.org/wiki/Reggie_Jackson).

Grade Placement for Newly Enrolled Students

There are some other points I need to make about determining grade placement for the student population you are going to serve, the lottery and eventual enrollment. Your particular circumstances will determine any/all matters concerning entry into your school; whether you are all-inclusive or have some type of placement testing (state law will very likely determine this). No child has ever been refused enrollment into any school I have worked at, however, their grade placement has at times been dependent upon first taking a placement test. If you arbitrarily enroll interested students into the grade their traditional public schools say they are at when they show up at your door, you may have a problem when you soon thereafter learn (most likely via a very frustrated teacher) that they are, in reality, at least a year, behind. It does no student any good to enroll in a grade in your school where they are doomed to fail from the start. I would never deny a student a classroom seat; only promote the idea that they should be placed at their appropriate level of academic performance, if possible. As the inheritor of many, many students who attended traditional public schools, where they were failures, I have found that after a year of great teaching their academic problems were most often no more. This comment is based on sixteen years of experience in charter schools. Note: there may be exceptions to placement decisions, e.g. for children with documented learning disabilities.

More on Placement

My past experience has indicates that when a recommendation is made to a parent that their child needs to repeat a grade, there is little resistance if the conversation is handled correctly. When the end of the next school year comes and this same student is fully successful, the parents know that the team decision was indeed the right one. As stated, I would never use a placement test to keep a student out of a school; but as a tool to determine present academic achievement level. If a student and their parent accept a lower grade placement then a regular public schools proposes they be promoted to, be sure and identify this student as having the need for assistance from your school's guidance counselor and, if appropriate, a Response to Intervention (RTI) teacher. Since all of us are carrying the banner for reforming public schools in this country, it becomes an imperative, literally, that no child is left behind.

Lottery

Included in most, if not all charter schools, is the issue of a need for a lottery, when there are more students interested in enrolling in your school then you have open seats. There are numerous ways to conduct a lottery, to include pulling numbers out of a jar (pretty primitive, but legal), using a "bingo-type" machine to pull numbered balls out of a cage, or using a computerized system. All will work when you need them to and some are more time consuming than others, the key is being sure nothing could ever appear to be "rigged" or biased. For the past three years at my current school, we have used the "bingo-type" machine to determine who is saved a classroom seat, with extra balls, of course, drawn after those who do get in, to establish a waiting list.

I highly recommend that you identify, well ahead of time, which students are siblings and who are boys or girls, or you are going to have a serious problem. I have no doubt you will find that some names are confusing and could represent either gender, so you should get this information straight before conducing the lottery. And, when I mention siblings, don't forget that in today's society there are going to be children in the same family with different last names, so be careful! Yes, we have "goofed up" on a couple of occasions, but were always able to do what we had to do (in one case add another student to a class that was technically full) because we made the error. Any decision you make should always give the parent the benefit of any doubt. You make mistakes, you learn from them, and you move on.

CHAPTER 3

Founders/Board of Directors/ Governance/Politics

This chapter will cover a number of topics and refers to the politics of the job of being a school administrator at a charter school in America today. I will do my best not to insult anyone here, but provide real world experiences and, if I get it right, help you avoid the many pratfalls that can contribute to the end of one's career as a charter school leader. I will not "name any names," this is not a personal vendetta, but my contribution to your success at your charter school.

As the senior school administrator in a charter school, there are numerous "types" of board members you may be dealing with. I will provide you with examples of some of the different types either I have served for or been advised about by other school leaders. For your information, on each type of board described there were parents; so I want to make it quite clear that I do not consider having parents on the board to be an inherent weakness, for, in fact, they can be a great plus to a board's effectiveness.

Type I: One Dominant Board Member

In Type I there is one dominant board member, most likely the Board Chair. This individual could very likely be in power at the very beginning because the idea for the charter school was theirs or they used a lot of their own political connections or money to influence the granting of the charter. This board member is going to continue to exact their influence on school outcomes, no matter who else is on the board. It is also quite possible this type of board chair will be continue to be reelected as Board Chair as the years go by, since no other board members have enough courage to challenge their authority, as stated granted by either money or other influence at the local community level or higher. What can happen in this instance is that once the school is on its way to success and there is no longer any need for a really strong board chair, they may start to use their position of original, willingly-granted power, to continue the appearance of power. This can take form in the hiring of "friends" without consideration for the needs of the school or in contracting with firms that would not normally be chosen to work with the school. As a school leader, you will have the choice to either go along, or move along.

Type II: Board with No Educational Experience, But Well-Intended Members

In this type of board, there may be some really nice people serving on the board, but without anyone with a background in education, you need to be prepared to plan and then ask for permission to implement any major educational decisions. I highly recommend that in a situation like this you use your networking skills to vet important decisions by your charter school administrative peers prior to presentation to your board. If you have previous experience in charter schools and know your business, you will be able to handle your decision-making role more confidently.

Type III: Board with Educated Members, Non-Educators, With Personal Agendas

Whereas having board members with a wide variety of educational backgrounds can certainly be considered a plus, when none of them have any background in education, but have their own ideas about how a charter school should be run, in particular in regard to the daily operation of the school, you are going to have a major problem. When your board is made up of "professional people," ones that have a day-day job of their own, they have plenty to do other than just attending your monthly board meetings. When you end up with a board composed of a high percentage of unemployed people, you may be asking for trouble. When board members have nothing else better to do in a day than come to the school and "snoop around," I predict you are going to experience a high degree of difficulty in keeping and maintaining staff morale at a high level since they will be acutely aware they are being "watched" for their effectiveness by someone other than a school administrator. The presence of board members on campus, on a continuing basis, identifies they are there for their own personal agenda, in particular when they appear at school unannounced, followed by "stop by requests" to speak to the Principal. The more board members you have with a personal agenda, e.g. those who want to reward teachers who show their children preference versus those who don't, the more difficult your job will be.

Type IV: Board Made Up of Business Professionals and Educators

When your board is made up of business professionals, to include those in finance and human resources, with an attorney thrown in, consider yourself extremely lucky. My preference for board governance is that proposed in "Charter School Board University: An Introduction to Effective Charter School Governance" (Carpenter, 2007). With Carpenter's recommended type of board governance policy, the school leader is really in charge; but along with the leadership role comes responsibility for whatever is happening in the school on a daily basis, either positive or negative. This is challenge I have always been very willing to accept. The reality is that as the leader of your charter school you will either meet or not meet expectations: students will either continue to make improvements in their achievement levels; the school budget will be managed professionally; and the students, parents and the staff and faculty will appreciate having you as their school leader. When you have these types of interpersonal stakeholder relationships and a solid, supportive relationship your board, serving as a charter leader can be a truly wonderful experience. This is not to say that you will never be challenged or questioned as to your rationale for making a decision or recommendation, only that they will show you the professional respect you are due when taking your proposal under consideration.

Ideal Board Composition:

There are lots of propositions about the make-up of an ideal board of directors. Most charter school administrators would agree that it is always a good idea to have at least one former/retired teacher or school administrator on the board. Some other desirable characteristics for board members include successful business experience, banking or financial background, fund raising experience and/or an attorney with labor relations experience.

CHAPTER 4

Choosing a Curriculum

What is a charter school? Everyone will have their own subjective opinion, most likely determined by their own personal perspective or by what they have either read or heard. The South Carolina Public Charter School District (SCPCSD) (www. sccharter.org) defines a charter school as "mission-driven." I absolutely concur with this statement, because a charter school's curriculum will almost always be determined by its mission and/or vision statement. On the same website, the SCPCSD also refers to charter schools as being "de-regulated, independent public schools of choice." These school attributes provide charter school administrators with the opportunity to employ a curriculum uniquely suited to the needs of their particular school population. Charter school authorizing authorities may come from a variety of sources, to include traditional public school districts, an institution of higher learning (IHE) or a state office of charter schools. Whoever the authorizer is, that approving authority usually sets the standard for charter school operation under their purview. The reality is, from my experience, that authorizing authorities find it easier to open charter schools than close them once they are in operation.

The Newcomer in Curriculum:

The initial response to nationwide implementation of Common Core College and Career Readiness Standards (http://www.corestandards.org/read-the-standards) seemed to be one of embracement, with forty-four states signing on for adaptation (http://corestandards.org/standards-in-your-state), however this trend later turned into questioning and, in some states, downright revolts. What is clear at this time (certainly in the State of South Carolina) is that educators are not being given clear-cut guidance on exactly what "part" of the Common Core Standards will be used for state testing purposes. The end result is that teachers may be required to teach to both Common Core and their individual state standards. If you are starting a charter school, the issue of curriculum may end up being one that "makes or breaks" you.

There are many different academic curricula being used in charter schools throughout the United States. Listed below are a few the ones I am most familiar with. This is not intended to be an all-inclusive list.

Blended Learning: On Rocky Mount Prep's website (www.rmp.org) it refers to itself as an "innovative hybrid school." Furthermore, under the topic of Accelerating Achievement with Blending Learning on this website, that blended learning:

> "combines the best of face-to-face learning with highly trained teachers using proven methods with the best of online learning using cutting-edge adaptive software programs that personalize instruction to each student's needs"

College Prep: The aim of college prep programs is "to increase college access, particularly for those students who are least likely to enroll" (http://ncsl.org/research/education/college-preparatory-programs-types-of-programs.aspx). In the past decade, college prep programs have sprung up at many new charter schools, in particular at those with a high percentage of high poverty/low income schools. Schools with college prep curriculums, like my own middle school, often participate in the federal government's Title I Free and Reduced lunch program.

Core Knowledge: Schools utilizing the Core Knowledge model operate on the premise that a grade-by-grade core of common knowledge" is needed to ensure that elementary school students in our country receive a proper education (http://en.wikipedia.org/wiki/Core_Knowledge_Foundation). The Core Knowledge wesbsite (www.coreknowledge.org/benefits-of-core-knowledge) promotes several advantages for schools that use its' program, to include: providing a plan for coherent, sequenced learning from grade to grade; promoting teamwork and an institution-wide focus; and enabling schools to work more efficiently while meeting and exceeding state standards.

Comment: My school utilizes the Core Knowledge curriculum, which I have no doubt has contributed significantly to our school's continuing success. While attending the "Innovative Practices for Charter Schools" course at Harvard University in 2010, my many collegial exchanges with other participants brought to my attention that a very high number of them use the Core Knowledge curriculum, frequently citing it as the driving force behind their school's overall success. These schools ranged from one's having little diversity to those designated as Title I schools; yet all enjoyed one thing in common, they achieved a very degree of academic success.

Cyber/On-Line Learning: There are numerous cyber/on-line charter schools throughout the United States, with the great majority of them (to include all of them in South Carolina) being operated by educational management organizations (EMO's). Students enrolled in on-line charter schools attend class primarily via computer-based delivery. According to information provided on the website of Provost Academy, an on-line charter school in South Carolina, students may attend class in a "synchronous" manner via live meetings on-line or through an entirely self-paced "asynchronous" means (www.provostacademy.com).

Inquiry-Based Learning: In an article titled "Concept to Classroom" at ThirteenEdOnline" (http:www.thirteen.org/edonlline/concept2class/inquiry/index_sub1.html) it states that "the inquiry approach is more focused on using and learning concepts as a means to develop information-processing and problem-solving skills." According to the article, inquiry-based learning is more student-centered, with the teacher serving more as a facilitator than instructor, therefore "how we come to know" is more important than "what we know." Proponents of this curricular category propose that the end result of inquiry-based learning is that students will be more interested and engaged in the classroom and that their skill development is on par with their understanding of content. My current school's mission statement notes inquiry-based teaching methodology as an integral part our academic identity.

Philosophy for Children: The Philosophy for Children curriculum was developed at Montclair State University in New Jersey. The professors who developed this program propose that "philosophy, among other things, is self-conscious inquiry into the meaning of puzzling and contestable concepts" (http:www.montclair.edu/cehs/academics/centers-and-institutes/iapc/what-is). It noted on this website that the founders of the Philosophy for Children curriculum (which is used in schools throughout the world) believe that "through the process of reading institute-prepared stories, students will learn to recognize ethical problems, to think them though, make sound ethical judgments and then take an appropriate action."

Montessori Education: Developed by the Italian physician and educator Maria Montessori, this curricula is "characterized by an emphasis on independence, freedom within limits, and respect for a child's natural psychological, physical, and social development" (http://en.wikipedia.org/wiki/Montessori_education). Furthermore, the Association Montessori Internationale (AMI) cites the following elements as being essential for a Montessori education (AMI School Standards) (http://amiusa/org/ami-slchools/ami-school-standards):

- Children 2 ½ to 3 to 6 years attend class in mixed age classrooms
- There is a high degree of student choice for activities
- Designed to have uninterrupted blocks of work time (ideally three hours)
- Utilization of a "discovery" model, where students work with concepts rather than hearing direct instruction from teachers
- Using specialized materials as designated by Montessori or her collaborators
- Freedom for students to move around the classroom
- Having a Montessori-trained teacher in the classroom

Note: There are also other specific Montessori-recommended guidelines for children age six, which can be located at (http://www.montessori-namta.org/Index.php. According to Wikipedia (http://en.wikipedia.org/wiki/Montessori Education) Montessori middle and high school programs are less developed than programs for younger children. According to Beth Love (personal communication, October 21, 2014), a middle school teacher at the Montessori Academy in Spartanburg, South Carolina, their middle and high school programs are targeted toward improving the abstract thinking of their young adolescents through project-based learning. According to Ms. Love, while her middle school students do, at times, use traditional textbooks, they very often participate in field trips to further emphasize what they have studied in class, e.g. after reading about world religions, students visited a Christian church, a Buddhist Temple and a Jewish synagogue. She adds that they also focus on community service, such as providing assistance to a local animal shelter.

Paideia: The Paideia Institute at the University of North Carolina at Chapel Hill states that this method of teaching "celebrates the fundamental notion that to be fully educated is a lifelong adventure that only begins with an individual's formal schooling" (www.learnnc.org/glossary/Paideia). One of my teacher training goals is to have all of my teachers familiar with Paideia teaching methodology. This website lists three instructional methods that guide activities: didactic instruction, coaching and the Paideia Seminar itself. A big change from the traditional teaching model, using the Paideia philosophy, only 10-15% of instructional time is allotted for direct instruction or what might be termed by many as teacher-delivered information.

S.T.E.M. Schools: "STEM is an acronym referring to the academic disciplines of science, technology, engineering, and mathematics" as it applies curriculum choices in educational settings" according to Wikipedia (http://wikipedia.org/wiki/STEM fields). Wikipedia notes the STEM concept began as a result of education and immigration debates about our countries lack of qualified candidates "for high tech jobs." The new emphasis on STEM schools is very likely related to the fact the U.S. ranked 12th out of 16 peer countries in proportion of STEM graduates (http://www.conferenceboard.ca/hcp/details/education/graduates-science-math-computer-science-engineerin.aspx).

Other curricular programs in this country include, but are not limited to, the following:

Basic Skills
Character Education
Coalition of Essential Schools
Community Service
Cooperative Learning
Direct Instruction
Distance Learning
Edison Project
Experiential Learning
International Baccalaureate
KIPP Academies
Multiple Intelligences
Reggio Familia
SABIS
Visual and Performing Arts

Evaluation of a School's Progress

Once your charter school is up and running, hopefully with great success, it will be time for what I categorize "due recognition." There are numerous ways to generate good publicity for your charter school, to include being designated by the federal government or a national non-profit organization as a "Blue Ribbon School." Another avenue for noting school success can be realized when your school receives accreditation by Advanc-Ed (formerly known as "SACS").

U.S. Department of Education Blue Ribbon Schools Program

As noted on the National Blue Ribbon Schools Program website (http://www.2ed. gov/programs/nclbbrs/index.html) this program recognizes "public and private elementary, middle and high schools based on their overall academic excellence or their progress in closing achievement gaps among student subgroups." This website notes that "more than 7,500 schools across the country" have been designated as National Blue Ribbon Schools. According to the website, this award "affirms the hard work of students, educators, families and communities in creating safe and welcoming schools where students master challenging content." A list of 2014 National Blue Ribbon Schools Program winners may be found on a link located at the website cited above. Public schools are normally nominated at the state level by their department of education.

Blue Ribbon Schools of Excellence, Inc. (BRSE)

The non-profit BRSE was founded by CEO/President Bart Teal. The organization's purpose, according to Teal (personal communication, August 12, 2012) is to identify and select schools for recognition in one of four qualifying categories of achievement, which include "Aspiring School," "Points of Light School," Blue Ribbon Beacon School," and, finally, the top rated "Blue Ribbon Lighthouse School." The last school in my local area to receive the "Lighthouse" designation was Spartanburg High School in 2005. With this knowledge in mind, everyone at my school became determined to find out where our school's achievement level would fit into the Blue Ribbon Schools of Excellence achievement hierarchy. What I found personally interesting about this process was that the real emphasis by BRSE was not on giving out awards, but on orienting a school toward continuous school improvement.

The measurement criteria used by BRSE includes the use of nine major categories, to include "Student Focus and Support," "School Organization and Culture," "Challenging Standards and Curriculum," "Active Teaching and Learning," "Technology Integration," "Professional Community," "Leadership and Educational Vitality," "School, Family, and Community Partnerships," and "Indicators of Success." BRSE utilizes a very rigorous assessment process; one that requires the administration of on-line surveys to students, parents and staff and an on-site school visit by BRSE personnel. After the school's assessment process is complete and, if they receive recognition in one of the four categories, they are honored at the annual Blue Ribbon Schools "Blueprint for Excellence Conference" held each December (B.Teal, personal communication, August 13, 2012). As noted on the BRSE website, "an assessment does not imply or guarantee award eligibility" (www.blueribbonschools.com). For the past three years, this conference has been held at Disneyworld's Contemporary Resort in Florida.

Advanc-ED

According to the Advanc-ED website (www.advanc-ed.org) it was re-born in its current configuration "through a 2006 merger of the PreK-12 divisions of the South Central Association (NCA) and the Southern Association of Colleges and Schools (SACS)-and expanded through the addition of the Northwest Accreditation Commission (NWAC) in 2011."

On the Advanc-ED website cited above, it notes that their research indicates that every school requires the following: stable governance, management and leadership; a coherent course of study; a reliable system by which to assess students' progress; instructors who have a clear understanding of what they aim to teach, how, and why; and access to the resources they need.

At a school improvement briefing I attended at the offices of Spartanburg School District Three in October 2014, Dr. Darrell Barringer, Director of Advanc-ED for South Carolina, identified their Standards for Quality School Systems: Purpose and Direction; Governance and Leadership; Teaching and Assessing for Learning; Resources and Support Systems and Using Results for Continuous Improvement.

Whereas some charter schools might receive state accreditation as a result of being chartered in their state, others may not, which can heighten the importance of receiving recognition from a national level organization like Advanc-ED. At my previous charter school assignment, we successfully went through reaccreditation through Advanc-ED, while at my current charter school we scheduled for our on-site visit in January 2015. Whereas many public schools receive accreditation as a result of their district's designation, charter schools, as "stand alones" must seek it on their own.

CHAPTER 5

Developing a School Budget

I was fortunate enough to have worked on developing and implementing multi-million dollar budgets during my career in the Army, so I was not in shock when I was asked to propose a school budget at my first charter school leadership assignment in 1999. This was a "start-up" charter school I assumed leadership responsibility for in mid-March of the school's first year. I doubt that very few, if any of us, received an adequate education, in either undergraduate or graduate school, about how to how to deal with the actual budgetary process. Most school administrators obtain their expertise by looking at examples provided by financial management organizations or by "begging" a colleague at another charter school to show you theirs. It is for this reason that it is entirely appropriate to seek out examples of budgets formulated by "successful" charter schools that are already in operation. I strongly recommend you do not rely on "guesstimates."

"Flush" and "Pre-Flush" Charter School Financial Managers

Who you choose to be your school's leader will be the critical factor in your school's ability to achieve success because leading/managing a charter school mandates the ability of the person in charge to manage a budget. Bill Moser, CEO of Kelley-Moser Consulting, LCC, the largest charter school financial management firm in South Carolina, identifies two types of financial managers at charter schools, referring to their types as "Flush" and "Pre-Flush" (personal communication, B. Moser, September 20, 2012). He clarified these titles by stating that a "Pre-Flush" financial manager always checks with his accounting firm before making any major purchase, in an effort to verify it has been listed as a budget line item and that there are sufficient funds remaining to make the expenditure. The "Flush" charter school financial manager, on the other hand, will spend money when they feel like it, which can definitely have a negative impact on the school's financial position. At one recent budget meeting, I was asked by one of my board members why our school was in such a good financial position. The only thing I could think of was "I'm a Pre-Flush Financial Manager." As a board of directors, you need to pay particular attention to the background of the person you hire as your school leader since budget management is just as important as their ability to be a successful curricular leader. The consequences of poor fiscal management can be disastrous. At least one charter school in South Carolina was closed in 2014 as a result of the alleged embezzlement of hundreds of thousands of dollars in federal and state funds.

Areas of Concern: Charter School Financial Management

No executive spending limits; no record of purchase orders; general poor bookkeeping techniques; no accountability between school administrators and accounting firm; having "in-house accounting;" charters managed by organizations with a "profit-first" corporate philosophy; charters embedded with religious agendas; and charter schools with great, idealistic intentions but no practical knowledge about what it takes to run a school.

If you are going to use another charter school's budget to project your own, be sure it accurately reflects the school's start-up year or successive ones since they can be distinctly different for reasons such as initial cost of moving into a facility, the necessary procurement of classroom furniture and "guestimates" of personnel costs (generally 50-60% of your total budget).

When I assumed leadership of my first charter school in Rocky Mount, NC in March of 1999, we were under the operational control of an Educational Management Company (EMO). With the flood destroying the school and ensuing budget issues in mind, the management company gave up on us, not believing that our vision of having a great charter school would ever come to pass. As a result of this mindset, my Board of Directors amicably severed ties with the EMO and went it on their own. To the surprise of many, and thanks to a $4.6 million dollar grant by FEMA in August of 2001, we moved into a new, built from the ground up, 70,000 square foot charter school (cost about $8 million).

The minute we opened, we were the largest charter school in the State of North Carolina, with about eight hundred students. That same year, the Director of Charter Schools in North Carolina at the time, Dr. Grova Bridges, referred to us as North Carolina's "Flagship Charter School" (G. Bridges, personal communication, 2001). Our monthly mortgage payment on the initial $3.4 million dollar mortgage was about $18,000 per month. Most notably, we never experienced a budget deficit while I was the school's senior school administrator; we always operated with a surplus (D. Leonard, personal communication, October 24, 2014).

I do not want to neglect to comment on the fact we provided bus transportation to and from school each day, from when we first opened at the Tarrytown Mall, to and from the mobile home site and later, at our permanent school location. With the great majority of our students coming from the urban population center of Rocky Mount, the school's survival depended on offering students a way to get and from our charter school. The last figure I can quote was that we were paying about $376,000 out of our yearly budget to provide transportation to our students (D. Leonard, personal communication, March 25, 2004). 2004 was my last year at this charter school. Since then, no charter school I have served at has provided bus transportation to its students. Rocky Mount Prep, in 2014, continues to do so, with its own fleet of busses (D. Haynes, personal communication, February 7, 2014).

In my next charter school leadership assignment, I served as Principal at a charter school in Central North Carolina, one that was so cash-strapped when I took over that it came close to me having to personally approve the purchase of pencils (this is really not too much of an exaggeration!). Why such a problem? It was because the school had shelled out so much money for renting the school facility, to include the modular I was located in, there was little left in the budget for anything other than salaries. While at this school we never ended up with a budget deficit at the end of the fiscal year, but did spend literally every dollar allotted (F. Shelton, personal communication, August 5, 2014). We used an in-house staff member for financial management and she did a truly commendable job. Many charter schools in the Carolinas use financial management firms to do their accounting. I strongly recommend you seriously consider out-sourcing your accounting needs unless you have close to a "CPA-qualified person" on hand to take care of your accounting needs.

One day while sitting in my office in the modular (an 8' x 8' room), the new Director of Charter Schools in North Carolina, Jack Moyer, called to advise me of a school leadership opening at a high achieving charter school in the rural, high poverty level part of the state. This K-8 charter school had a fixed student population of five hundred students and a hard to believe waiting list of five hundred local students! The school qualified for supplemental state funds due to its designation as "low wealth county," a result of the relocation of the textile industry overseas and a reduction in tobacco dependence (J. Moyer, personal communication, January 11, 2006).

Jack strongly recommended I follow up on his referral. After going through the interview process, I decided to take the job, looking for another challenge in my career. We were fortunate at this charter school in that we had very low overhead since the school was located in what used to be the entrance, main hallway, lobby and interior of a now-closed J.C. Penny store and some other defunct small businesses, to include a shoe repair. The total square footage was around 58,000 square feet and we only paid about $13,700 per month in rent. The Board of Directors had spent several hundred thousand dollars to renovate the building before moving into the facility in 1999. If you haven't heard, there is an unwritten "law" in charter schools that once you have four hundred or more students under your purview, your economy of scale reaches a point where you can begin to generate a surplus and have money available to purchase items previously categorized as non-essential.

During my four years at this charter school, almost $900,000 in surplus funding was saved toward the construction of a new school facility. In 2009, an architect was hired to design a new school, while additional efforts were made to find available property to build on. These plans were presented to the board of directors before I departed in 2010. I would be remiss if I failed to point out that this K-8 charter school produced some of the highest achieving middle school graduates in rural North Carolina, with several of them being accepted into Raleigh Charter High School, a 2014 designee as a United States Department of Education "Blue Ribbon School" (www.newsobserver. com/2014/09/30/4195388_two-triangle-schools-win-national-html?rh=1). If you have come to the conclusion that charter schools have to be very careful with their money, in particular in regard to saving for a new school facility, you are absolutely correct. When you do have a surplus, it is quite difficult to complain about underfunding when you do not spend the money allocated to you.

Why would anyone ever leave a school that was academically flourishing, one where you had a great staff and five hundred highly motivated students and wonderful, supportive staff? The answer is quite simple, after three years developing budgets, presenting them to the Board of Directors and being responsible for producing a significant financial surplus, the make-up of the board changed dramatically and new members of the Board of Directors took over budget planning. Please read the section on "Politics" to understand why my departure followed, with a full year's notice. I would like to point out the Board of Directors had my replacement chosen from my staff by December of that year, 2009, so a transition plan was already in place when I left. As with the majority of charter schools in the North Carolina, financial management services were provided by a financial management firm. I left the school in great financial condition, with a surplus close to $900,000.00.

While I was still living in rural North Carolina and interviewing for my next school leadership position, I received a telephone call from one of the founders of Spartanburg Charter School (later renamed Spartanburg Preparatory School – SPS) located in downtown Spartanburg, South Carolina. Since I loved the

Carolinas from my military days at Fort Jackson, near Columbia and saw a lot of potential in this particular charter school setting, I accepted the position, knowing it was in its initial start-up phase. From August to March of that first year the school had been led by a group of school founders and staff members, none of whom had any experience operating any type of school. Does this sound familiar? Within three weeks of my arrival, around the first week of April 2010, at my first budget meeting at this school (an emergency one at that), one of the board members present asked what then seemed like the fatal question, "Does Dr. von Rohr know he might not have a job three months from now?" At that time, the less than twelve charter schools in the South Carolina Public Charter School District were receiving a mere pittance of $2,300 per student, period. This is not anywhere near enough to pay all the bills and keep the doors open. It was realistically projected that we would be out of money by February 2011, and have no choice but to close the doors of the school.

What actually happened was that in October of 2010, we won $500,000 in Kohl's Department Store contest, which carried us over until the end of the 2010-2011 school year, at which time state funding was increased to about $5,000 per pupil, enough to make everyone optimistic about the schools' financial future. From 2011 to present, state funding has increased to about $5,700 per student, still well short of what our neighboring traditional public school receives (about $11,000 per pupil) but enough, with our conservative spending in effect, to remain operationally functional. As the Principal, I answer to my board of directors for any unbudgeted spending, which is why I budget carefully in the first place.

CHAPTER 6

Hiring Administrators

The Four Tests

Charter school founders and school board will, in general, experience great joy when they find a competent charter school administrator. After speaking with a group of elite charter school leaders at a national conference at Harvard University in 2010, I came to the conclusion there is a distinct, nation-wide shortage of public school candidates who really know what it takes to successfully operate a charter school.

How do you identify the most qualified candidate among applicants? I propose that there are four "Tests" that will assist you in this task. They consist of "Exhibited Financial Management," "Documented Leadership," "Vision" and "Personality/Ability to Think Out of the Box."

Test One – Exhibited Financial Management

A charter school leader wears many more "hats" than their traditional public school counterpart, in particular when it comes to having a "business sense." Yes, I said "business," because in charter schools the great majority of Principals also serve as the school's overall business manager. Unlike traditional public school leaders, those who lead charter schools do not have a budget provided to them by district personnel; they actually have to prepare and propose a budget to their board of directors and then, once approved, fiscally operate within its established parameters.

Once, while in the Army during the Gulf War conflict, serving as the Police Chief on a military reservation, I was advised we were receiving a $1 million dollar grant to upgrade our security posture on base. With the knowledge that this was taxpayers money we being given, I spent $30,000 on concrete barriers and about $300 on mirrors to look under cars for explosives when they entered the military installation; then returned the remainder of the funds to Department of the Army.

Can you figure out the message here? It would be quite rare for someone to suddenly give you an extra $1 million dollars to spend once your charter school budget has been set, therefore a charter school leader must learn to function within the budget that receives final approval by their board of directors. Failure to live within your means could result in bankruptcy or having the school's charter pulled by the authorizing authority.

If you have the luxury of finding a candidate for your school leadership position that already has charter school leadership that reflects their ability to manage large budgets effectively, they have passed the first test.

Test Two – Documented Leadership

In reality, the number of school administrators who can honestly check off a block marked "successful charter school leadership" are few and far between, however they are out there, somewhere, but you may have to dig deep to find them. One of the best sources for finding charter school leadership talent could be your highest ranking state charter school official, whether this individual has the title of "Superintendent' or "Director" makes no difference, it is likely they are aware of potential candidates who could serve you well or hurt you. Corporate head hunters are another source for school directors; this is how I ended up in my first charter school leadership position. I will comment more on "head hunters" shortly.

Quite honestly, I had never served in a charter school before 1999; my experience had been gained at the college level, at a traditional public high school and a private K-8 school. I have no doubt that my past military experience has played a significant role in my success as a charter school leader. Keeping in mind that stereotyping all former military officers as good leaders, I have read of numerous instances where school districts hired retired general officers (that is of the rank of "Brigadier General" or higher) to be their Superintendents. From my personal perspective, I would have liked to have seen these high ranking persons "pay their dues" in educational settings before inheriting these positions, but here is no doubt that their ability to run large organizations often carried over into their public school successes. It is not my general intent to recommend to you that you hire a retired general to be your school leader; that would very likely be "overkill," however considering a person with past military experience could turn out to be a positive.

After you have spoken to a lot of people in the charter school universe, in particular those who have time and time again been able to produce results of a high-achieving nature, you will most likely find they will have one thing in common; they have mentored a group of people who are potential candidates for your school leadership position. Each and every one of my teachers who later became an Assistant Principal later went on to lead their own school as a Principal; with all of them proving their value to the charter school board they ended up serving.

If you can verify that a candidate already has a proven track record of success at a charter school in your state or another one with similar laws, it would make sense for you to approach them. It might be for reason of more money, or, more altruistically, a desire to take on a new challenge that encourages them to apply for your open position.

Test Three – Vision

Any truly interested candidate will do research on your school before you interview them. If you are in a start-up status, this may be difficult or impossible;

however, you should ask them about where they would see themselves in the future as your school leader. If they have previously served as Principal or Assistant Principal at a highly successful traditional charter school or charter school, they should have a well-developed concept of how their leadership abilities can move your student body population to a high achieving status. It is important to remember it is not where you start, but where you intend to finish. When you hire a school leader that only has traditional public school experience, their learning curve is going to be much steeper, but the ability to lead people should not be disregarded under any circumstances. If you do hire an applicant from a traditional public school system, I strongly recommend you employ a person that has produced high achievers, taking student growth models into consideration. Hiring an individual who has not been successful at a traditional public school is not going to benefit you; in fact, they will very likely be even more confused than anything else since charter school leadership may overwhelm them. In my opinion, the duty requirements of a charter school administrator far exceed those of their public school counterparts.

Test Four – Personality/Ability to Think "Out of the Box"

Charter schools are, by their very nature, "different," so your search for a school leader needs to reach out for someone other than the traditional school leader "type," or at least a candidate that possesses some unique personality characteristics. Your search should seek to find a person who is outgoing and willing to get involved with your stakeholders. In some traditional public schools, parents often have inconsequential contact with the very person that makes daily decisions that impact their child's life. Charter school leaders must be problem solvers if they are going to be successful. As an example, you can forget the "I'll get back to you within 24 hours" message you so often hear on public school administrator voicemails. Charter schools leaders should subscribe to my adage "a fire does not go out if you throw gasoline on it" and provide a higher degree of personal responsiveness.

Whomever you select as your charter school leader, they need to know, in advance, what is expected of them in regard to parent requests for communication. I have never felt quick response time to parents was hoped for, but that it was always an expectation for the job. Since as charter school people we do not normally have all of the bureaucratic "layers" that exist in regular public schools, with no district offices to deal with (unless you are chartered by a local school district), there is no excuse for slow communication with parents, so once again, a candidate for this job must be not only professional but willing to make as new "path" when it comes to communication with the parents they serve. Whomever you select needs to understand this expectation for leadership of your charter school.

There is undoubtedly one more question in your mind. I propose that question is "who should be making the decision about who leads our school?" In almost all cases, any final decision about who becomes the school's leader will come from a charter school's board of directors. Searches for school leaders can be made at the local, state, national or even international levels, by your own board of directors or by what are commonly referred to as "headhunter firms" such as Carney, Smith & Sandoz Associates. I secured my first charter school leadership position in 1999 after answering an advertisement in a weekly educational publication.

In the years that have followed, I have become good friends with this firm's Senior Search Consultant, Barry Rowland, who is works out of their Toronto, Canada office. When Barry learned I was writing this book, he expressed an interest in its contents (B. Rowland, personal communication, September 2, 2014) and was gracious enough to forward to me his firm's document titled "The Successful School Leadership Search." The Table of Contents for this document includes such topics as "Why Hire a Search Consultant?" If you are considering a national level search for a school leader, I highly recommend you contact Barry at (www.carneysandoe.com).

Most people starting up a charter school have either no idea who to contact to lead their school or they have a local educator in mind. Please, if you are going to hire a former traditional public school employee to lead your charter school, be sure they possess the skills to lead in a truly unique setting, acknowledging that leading in one school environment does not necessarily guarantee success in the other.

As you will likely find out for yourself, finding a pool of well qualified charter school administrators may be quite challenging. I want to add that personal friendships have no place when it comes to hiring a school administrator; all decisions should be made with the school's needs, not yours, as an individual board member, in mind. On this same topic, if you are going to conduct a candidate search, do just that, don't bring in a group of candidates from out of town for what was referred to in my Army days as a "dog and pony show," just to give the impression of a fair and impartial search.

CHAPTER 7

Hiring Teaching Staff

Over the years I have witnessed numerous "processes" for hiring teachers at charter schools, to include using "rotating group interviews" (4-7 people interview, followed by a break and then interviews continue with another group of 4-7 people, etc.), small group interviews (2-3 people, e.g. Principal, Assistant Principal and a teacher), and a one person interview by the senior administrator (Principal) where this one person interviews and then selects the teacher to be hired.

I have seen all three processes work, however, you should recognize that as a charter school administrator you are going to have a lot more personal interaction with your staff, meaning you won't be able to "blame" the school district's human resource (HR) department for hiring a "bad apple," therefore, as Principal, I am **always** involved in the hiring of teaching staff. A great staff is what really makes the difference!

The other side of the coin here is that as a Principal, you will very likely be the one that informs non-performers they are not being rehired (another word for "terminated"). As the senior school administrator, I willingly assume this responsibility, so I do my very best to bring in new staff members who will be a good fit with my particular leadership style and charter school requirements.

If you're not good at interviewing, you need to obtain the assistance of someone who possesses both good common sense and intuition. I do prepare questions before I interview candidates, but have found that you tend to get "canned" responses when you ask traditional questions like "Why would you like to teach at this school?" I also tend to avoid asking teaching candidates about their biggest strength or weakness, since answers to these questions do not necessarily provide insight and are most often prepared beforehand. Your charter school is unique, so be bold, different and surprise teaching candidates with some really meaningful questions!

I routinely ask candidates if they know what a charter school is and why they would like to teach at my school versus a traditional public school. The information I obtain from their answers lets me know if they did their "homework" before coming to the interview and, in particular, if they realize the type of educational environment they would be committing themselves to.

Salaries

The issues of salary and benefits will be of vital concern to anyone who is considering applying to your school for a staff position, whether it be for instructional staff or otherwise. Many have asked why schools under my leadership have done so well. My answer is not at all complicated: I hire the best people and pay them what they are worth. If you are really trying to hire the highest quality instructional staff, those who will carry your charter to "academic glory," it is not going to be cheap. Appling the old adage "you get what you pay for" certainly applies here. Hiring a majority of unproven, first year teachers is not going help you reach the upper rung of academic success quickly and/or in a necessarily timely manner. This is not to imply a "mix" of experienced and new teachers is not a good idea, for it is an entirely reasonable one; just that not ALL of your teachers should be first year teachers. I not only pay my staff what they would earn if employed in the seven adjoining school districts, but offer them the possibility of a bonus (determined by my board of directors each year if the school continues to perform at the "A" level for student achievement). This past year, my board also awarded a $500 "signing bonuses" to all instructional staff.

Benefits

Some charter schools are fortunate to have enough financial sponsorship to enable them to join their state's retirement system, while others can only afford to be part of their state's medical and dental programs. Available funding is going to decide this matter. I have experienced both options, being part of the statement retirement plan and not. If it is your board of director's decision not to become part of the state retirement system, I strongly recommend you have some form of financial incentive in place, like a 401(k) or 503(b), both which allow for pre-taxed income to go into individual retirement/investment accounts. If you take this option, contact with several investment firms is advisable.

Resume Review

The resumes of potential teacher candidates should be examined very closely, in particular for "job hopping" and other periods of short-term employment, along with the traditional review of teaching credentials. Frequent job changes could indicate something as simple as moving because a spouse changed jobs, their personal inability to perform their teaching duties successfully at a particular school, or a lack of flexibility to adjust to a new school climate. When a teaching candidate has not listed some type of school administrator, e.g. Assistant Principal or Principal as a reference, my warning antenna goes up. Under normal circumstances, if a school administrator is not listed, I will routinely call an identified school to speak to the Principal, if possible, to determine the teacher's on the job performance at that school. If the teacher has not notified their current school that they are job-hunting, I will respect their situation and check with other references and use my personal intuition in reference to the possibilities of any unidentified issues at their current school. Teachers or department heads at their current school usually serve as good references in these circumstances and are often listed as alternative sources of information.

By utilizing this practice of conducting reference checks, I have identified teachers who were arrested and terminated; one identified as the father of a student's child and another, who was arrested for assaulting a police officer. It is good news indeed when senior school administrators provide glowing recommendations for teachers; I just like to be sure and not leave any rock unturned when it comes to knowing what I am getting. It is common knowledge that in many states charter school instructional staff are employed on year-to year contracts, in an "at will" status, that practice being commonplace here in South Carolina. I take my job as the senior hiring authority very seriously. A copy of a teacher contract is attached at Appendix J.

CHAPTER 8

Hiring for Key Staff Positions

Special Education Director

If you fully expect your charter school to be successful, you need to pay particular attention to who you hire as your Special Education Director. The person in this position can either "make or break you" when it comes to compliance with federal and state regulations that pertain to students with disabilities. For two years at my current school I was in almost weekly contact with our charter school district due to concerns about the presentation of proper paperwork to them from my Special Education Director. This is not to say that services were not being provided to our students as mandated by their Individual Education Plans (IEP's), but that these services were not being properly documented. Did this give me headaches as a school leader? Absolutely, and it seemed to be a never-ending problem until I hired a new Special Education Director. Since the arrival of this new individual, our school has transformed itself from being merely "compliant" to being characterized by Dr. Robert Compton, Director of Federal Programs for the South Carolina Public Charter School District as "the model Special Education Program in the district" (R. Compton, personal communication, September 15, 2014). My advice on this topic is simple; take the time to check not only about a candidate's ability to direct the delivery of Special Education services, but to document them in an acceptable manner.

Business Manager

Hiring the right business manager could well determine your fate as a charter school leader or your school's ability to keep its door open. "Business Managers" seem to come in many different configurations, to include the extremes of "highly competent" and "incompetent." Most charter schools I am familiar with farm out their accounting needs to private financial management firms. In this situation, the duties of the Business Manager include collecting receipts payable (invoices) and forwarding them to the accounting firm for payment. In addition, under this format, the accounting firm pays the monthly salaries of your staff members, keeps up with what you are collecting and spending each month and prepares a monthly budget report for your board of directors. In other words, an agency outside your school keeps track of how you are spending funds compared to your projected budget.

The majority, by far, of charter schools I have served at have had a Business Manager like the one I have just described. An independent audit company reports on your financial management firm's handling of your money. Two of my former business managers, both of this type, are still close friends with me to this day, even though we worked together up to fifteen years ago. I owe lot of my success to these two ladies.

The second type of school financial management is in place when the Business Manager at your school personally receives all bills and pays them, in addition to doing monthly payroll. This individual prepares monthly financial reports for presentation to a board of directors. At one charter school I was senior administrator at our Business Manager was a true superstar. This does not appear to be a naturally-occurring phenomena and I am personally aware of several charter schools that closed when they had their finances done "in-house." Here is what I consider to be sound advice: do not hire a relative to do your accounting! I have personal knowledge that in several states charter schools have closed due extremely poor financial management, very often due to relatives "cooking the books" to make their family members look good, while at the same time embezzling thousands of dollars for themselves. In most states, to keep charter schools "honest," an independent firm conducts a yearly audit of all financial records.

Charter schools are not just educational institutions, they are also a business, and I therefore recommend you be very careful indeed about whom you hire; your career could depend on it. I strongly recommend that you pay close attention to the credentials offered to you by candidates for this position. And, if you are able to hire a really good person for this job, be sure and always let them know how much you appreciate them!

School Nurse

One way or the other, you are going to need a nurse at your school if you want to foster good parent-school relationships. In many states, nurse grants are available. When I think back on the past sixteen years, I recognize that when the student population at a charter school reaches 300 or more, a nurse becomes a necessity. When you hit that 300 count, the number of children to be assessed on a daily basis in the office for self-described illnesses can quickly overwhelm your administrative staff. This issue becomes even more complicated when there is a need to call parents and then have to answer any medically-oriented inquiries they might make.

You will need to check with your state department of education as to what their prerequisites are for a school nurse. Some states require a license Registered Nurse (RN), while in others a Licensed Practical Nurse (LPN) is sufficient. In South Carolina an LPN may serve as a school nurse as long as they have a legitimate RN as a contact point for emergencies. In addition to being an LPN, my current nurse also holds certification as an Emergency Medical Technician (EMT).

School nurses will be doing a lot more for you than just checking children's temperatures, to include taking body fat measurements for government studies on student obesity rates and doing hearing and vision screenings. Most importantly, in the event of an accident on the playground, your school nurse can perform legitimate triage at a level your office personnel cannot. School liability is a serious matter to take into consideration when making your decision on this matter, keeping in mind that being the defendant in a lawsuit is never a pleasant experience.

Another factor, often forgotten by many of us, is staff health as an issue. In 2013, one of my teachers had a heart attack at school, in a second floor classroom, while students were downstairs at lunch. Some details: While in my office, at about 12:15 P.M. one school day, I heard a female scream, after which I ran down the hallway to find our beloved science teacher on his back, face up, on the classroom floor, unresponsive. My school nurse arrived at the classroom location within one minute, which brings up another important good point; be sure you have a good communication system within your school in the form of both an intercom system and/or walkie-talkies (ones that really work!).

You can call the following either professional or personal advice, but having staff, to include school administrators, certified in CPR techniques, is CRITICAL. I sincerely hope that you never have to experience what I did that day, but, what in reality happened was that while my school nurse worked on restoring his breathing, I was doing chest compressions. In the minutes that followed, other staff members assisted, either in offering direct assistance or by making needed emergency telephone calls and/or notifications. The amount of teamwork displayed by each and every staff member showed that our crisis management plan worked. EMT's arrived shortly thereafter but, unfortunately after about an hour, we learned that our friend had passed away on the trip to the hospital. As school leader, your Principal may have some pretty tough duties; mine that day was to contact both his wife and mother to advise them that he had passed away.

What could have been done differently? It took me a long time to answer this question, but, with my School Nurse's input, one specific recommendation was presented to us; have an Automatic Emergency Defibrillator (AED) on hand in your charter school facility. We always think about our students, but we need to remember we have staff members too, many of whom may have personal, undiagnosed medical issues. The cost for an AED is not cheap ($1,500.00), but if you only need to use it one time and it saves just one life, it has paid for itself.

School Counselor

Of the four charter schools (three start-ups, one established) I've worked at in the past sixteen years, all but one did not have a school counselor on staff. This exception was a K-8 school with about 500 students, in a very rural environment, with a great connection to local high schools for academic counseling and county mental health agencies for needs of that nature. This was a constant at my first start-up charter school; after moving into a permanent school facility, we did hire a school counselor, who was especially needed by students in our middle school and those who would be attending to our soon-to-be built high school.

I do support the proposition that society has become more complicated and, as the years have gone by, I have definitely seen an increase in the need for student counseling services, in particular to deal with poor interpersonal relationships among students, which can manifest themselves in the form of bullying and cyberbullying. A school counselor is, in many instances, the staff member best suited to fulfill the role of being the school's primary reporter of cases of suspected child abuse and/or neglect. The proper framework for reporting issues of this kind are discussed in Chapter 10, titled "Conducting Investigations in a School Setting."

If you are attempting to determine who would be an ideal candidate for your school's Testing Coordinator, I strongly recommend you look to your guidance counselor to fill this position. In my past experience, they have turned out to be highly reliable, trustworthy people.

Facilities Manager

I never had a Facilities Manager on staff until I took over the reins at what was then Spartanburg Charter School in 2010. Since the building was built in 1939, there were all kinds of mechanical issues that had to be resolved, to include an over seventy year old boiler; antiquated bathrooms; an elevator that at times did not work, but got "stuck" between floors with staff inside; a playground area that needed upgrading; general landscaping issues; hallways that needed renewal efforts; hardwood floors that needed re-finishing; window air conditioners that would eventually wear out; almost a hundred windows that were going to have to be replaced; and a cafeteria air conditioning system that was so old only a "very mature" electrician had had any idea how to fix it. If you find yourself in an older building, you are going to have on-going issues with repairs and/or replacement of items and operating systems to keep your school operating smoothly and keeping the doors open. Some advice: Be sure you put a reasonable amount of money in your budget for repair and/or replacement of HVAC systems.

Receptionist

Are you surprised I am taking the time to remark on the hiring of your receptionist? This is, absolutely, a "make or break" position on your staff. I propose that there are several key characteristics to look for in hiring for this position. The individual who serves as your school's "first-line of defense" should possess, at a minimum, the following capabilities and personality characteristics: the ability to quickly become knowledgeable about who is in your student population; be able to eventually identify their parents when they come to the school; possess the personal demeanor needed to remain calm and polite under some very trying circumstances; and have the common sense to know when to recommend to school administrators there is an imminent danger and it is time for a school-wide "lock down." In addition, to feel really comfortable as a school leader, it is imperative that you feel confident your school receptionist is well versed in the school's crisis management plan.

CHAPTER 9

Daily Operational Plans

One of the most important factors in the success of a charter school leader lies in their ability deal with a wide variety of staff, student and parent issues involving school policy that come up on an almost daily basis. I am, honestly, continually coming up with new "Daily Operational Plans," it seems like a never-ending requirement. The reason for these phenomena is quite simple; as times change, there is a measurable increase in the need to integrate technology into your decision making. The constant changes in the use social media are having a significant impact on communication that may begin far away from school, but result in very serious consequences on students under your supervision at school. Cyber bulling is a good example of social media's impact on society. Sample "Daily Operational Plans" are included at Appendix K.

Over the years, I have continually made additions and, as stated, I am not done yet. There are some you might not use; others you really need to have in place the first day your school starts. Through the insightful addition of Daily Operational Plans, you can save yourself a lot of trouble when the time comes by not having to say "Sorry, we don't have a policy for that yet."

CHAPTER 10

Conducting Investigations in a School Setting

A criminal investigator and a school administrator have similar jobs in that they are responsible for collecting facts in order to resolve problematic situations. Assuming that readers of this publication will not have any prior investigative experience, I will purposely keep things as simple possible so that both novice and experienced school leaders are able to learn and apply these lessons to their daily life as school administrators. What I have been able to determine from my two careers, the first in law enforcement, the second as a school administrator, is that while as a school administrator you may have been taught a lot about curriculum implementation and how to dish out consequences to wrong-doers, you received literally no direction, in either a college or university teacher education programs or in postgraduate educational leadership training, about how to properly investigate incidents of concern in a school setting, some of these events being of such a serious and overwhelming nature that they have the potential for making, or quickly ending a career in school leadership.

Throughout this book I will provide you with examples of the "do's" and "don'ts" involved in conducting investigations in an educational setting. I have done my best to provide real life scenarios as to how these principles should be applied. Whereas the reading of this book will not make you an "expert", I firmly believe that by applying some/many of the investigative techniques noted you will find your daily work life as a school administrator much more sustainable, with a new-found sense of confidence as a result of having this book as a resource when you need it. I have purposely attempted to inject humor into my writing to make your reading more entertaining and easy to digest, to avoid boring you with only a format for you to use. It is my opinion that when you can associate real life with theory, your learning curve will be shortened.

The Proper Mental State to Investigate an Offense

The duties of a criminal investigator and a school administrator are actually quite similar in nature since they have several common missions; to include identifying and locating the perpetrator of an offense and then providing evidence of guilt in one setting or the other. The ability to successfully investigate any alleged offense is much more of an "art" than a "science" no matter where you apply investigative techniques, otherwise everyone would be equally successful resolving complicated matters presented to them. However, even the most inexperienced school administrator can learn time-honored investigative techniques to the point they will be able to routinely resolve incidents that occur on their campuses.

The difference between achieving high or moderate success rate in these endeavors is often the result of, quite simply put, individual intuition and common sense. In reality, personal intuition often trumps the most modern, methodical scientific examination of an offense. The knowledge of even the most complicated crime scene techniques is of no use to you if you do not know the right questions to ask in the first place. What you need to be fully successful in conducting investigations in a school setting is a combination of knowing the general principles involved in conducting investigations and the personal fortitude to see an investigation through to its conclusion. This does not mean that every noted task has to be done entirely "by the book" every time, but that you do need to adhere to some fundamental prerequisites.

For anyone conducting investigations, the classic text is "Fundamentals of Criminal Investigation" (O'Hara & O'Hara, 2003). For an extremely detailed account of the "nitty-gritty" of conducting an investigation, I highly recommend this text as a resource guide.

While it would be wonderful to be able to claim that any offense committed on a school campus can be solved, it would be preposterous to state this, for no one solves every crime, no matter how proficient your investigative talents are. Your success rate should, however, be much higher as a result of the proper application of the investigate techniques I will be passing along to you. Your success as a school administrator could likely be determined by how proficiently you conduct your investigation of an alleged offense. This means that you did everything in your power to bring your investigation to a successful conclusion, to include if it means turning the control of the matter over to another investigative authority. In regard to this same point, it would be ridiculous to assume you are always going to have enough evidence to prove "who did what to whom," no one's luck is ever that good. At times, there is just not enough evidence to even prove an offense did or did not occur. You will not always "solve" a crime, because there are times when no crime occurred to begin with, however, you will have spent numerous hours of your work day investigating anyway. The positive part of this end result is that you will likely be able to determine that no offense was committed in the first place. Reference "evidence," in the form of eyewitnesses, motives or physical clues, they will not always there, so you will sometimes have to use your own personal intuition, rather than facts, to figure out what really happened. My advice is simple, do not assume anything and keep an objective, totally non-biased point of view, while seeking the truth; in particular when there are political implications.

The reality is that you will be rated by your superiors by how you handled any evidence you obtained, how well you interviewed available or later identified witnesses, whether or not you successfully interviewed your prime or secondary suspects and, finally, how good the report is that you tender to whomever you work for upon completion of your investigation.

The Importance of Good Documentation

I firmly agree with the old saying "if it is not documented it didn't happen." If you plan on lasting long as a school administrator in a charter school, it is imperative that you accurately document any investigations you conduct in a school setting, to include that you handed off any serious incidents to the proper authorities. This will save you lots of grief in the long run. The other advice involves noting the "who, where, when, what, how and why" in your documentation. It is definitely a good idea to train your staff in how to properly fill out disciplinary referral forms whenever disciplinary action is a possible consequence. It does not take a genius level intellect to prepare a preliminary incident report prior to forwarding to a school administrator.

I recommend the in-depth preparation of Memorandum for Records for any serious event reported to you; to ensure anyone inquiring about the event, in particular your Board of Directors, can easily determine you did a professional job of investigating.

Securing the Crime Scene

When you are first notified that an offense has occurred on campus you should keep in mind that whenever students are concerned there can be chaos in regard to the collection of any evidence. If there has been a serious physical assault, in particular, you should ensure that the scene is secured, immediately, and that any potential witnesses are isolated, individually, so that you can interview them without their testimony being contaminated by communicating with their fellow students. If wall lockers are an issue of concern with your investigation, assign someone to ensure they are not tampered with.

Any available evidence, to include surveillance videos, should be secured for your review. In my current school, we have video of the back playground area since that seems to be the place most, if any, physical aggression takes place, by young boys, at recess, in particular. Any cost for a video surveillance system will pay for itself the first time a parent claims "My son would never do that" and you can provide video evidence of the misbehavior. In my charter school in Rocky Mount, NC we also had video surveillance capabilities in the main hallways, which not only contributed to the overall security of our school, but kept students from engaging in certain misbehaviors since they knew the cameras were there. If financially feasible, I recommend cameras in the main hallways at the middle and high school grade levels.

Determining Investigative Responsibility

Whenever in doubt, call your local law enforcement authority; or, if when suspected child abuse or neglect is suspected, call the Department of Social Services (DSS) or your local equivalence. If an incident is serious enough to make you wonder who should be investigating, make that call. A key to your thought process should be asking yourself the simple question "Could someone go to jail for committing this offense?"

If the answer is yes, you need to figure out what you can legally do, versus what other authorities can accomplish. Your goal will always be to create an investigative plan and keep to it unless you find out there are mitigating circumstances that take the incident to a level above your pay grade as a public school administrator.

Searching for Evidence and Your Authority

As a charter school administrator, your position allows you to search student wall lockers with or without a student's permission/consent, however, I routinely ask a student for permission to search their locker; this is my personal preference, even in the instance where there is suspicion that drugs or a weapon are involved. Any evidence you find must be secured, immediately. This does not mean putting it in the top drawer of the desk in your office, but, more appropriately, in a locked file cabinet, where no one else has access to it. Weapons of any kind, i.e. plastic replica guns, knives of any kind (to include toys), throwing stars (yes, I've confiscated them from elementary students) or "real" weapons, need to be properly secured in the event they are turned over to law enforcement authorities. The police term for keeping evidence secured is referred to as the "chain of evidence." Losing evidence will make you look unprofessional, so be sure you secure it!

The Use of K-9's for a Search

It is never a bad idea for a charter school administrator to have a local enforcement agency bring a K-9 drug detection dog through the school building on an irregular schedule. A K-9 dog will reduce the possibility that students will bring drugs to school. If you are on top of what is going on in your school environment, the presence of K-9's in your building will be an infrequent occurrence. A recommended time for K-9 presence in your school facility might be during your yearly "Red Ribbon" week. Maybe I have been fortunate, but since 1999, no K-9 searches at any of my charter schools have turned up any drugs, but there is always a first time. Being proactive is the key to keeping any illegal substances out of your school.

Photographic Evidence at a Crime Scene

With the ready availability of smart phones in our society, I highly recommend you utilize them to take photographs of any evidentiary value, to include damage to school property and/or physical marks on any child's body as a result of an assault. Bruise marks, in particular, may disappear in a day, but a photograph of those marks on your smart phone (printed and transferred to your investigative file) proves that a picture is worth a thousand words." Photographs prove to be a necessity when you need proof an offense occurred.

Dealing With the Internet/Cyber Bullying

The latest legal ruling on the subject of internet bullying has most likely appeared in the latest issue of Legal Notes in Education (2014), which recently noted that if a student generates a threat or bullies another student via the internet, they are not immune from prosecution. In reality, we all know that social media is now used to express opinions not normally revealed in traditional person-to-person contact. From my personal experience, we now have a new generation of "bullies" in our schools, students who would not have in the past threatened anyone, but who now believe the internet and social media give them the opportunity to express their feelings without consequence. These beliefs are not accurate. It is, however, quite difficult to determine who sent whom to what as a result of the fact that many websites are being physically hosted outside the United States, therefore, obtaining a search warrant through national or international law enforcement agencies is quite time-consuming, or downright impossible.

When students readily identify themselves as bullies through social media, these "messages" can, under some circumstances, be used against them for purposes of disciplinary action. In addition, I am personally aware of an incident in which a parent expressed dissatisfaction with a teacher on Facebook, which was subsequently read by a person no longer associated with the school. This "reader" then remarked on this same website that they would be willing to "cut" the teacher originally being complained about. This posting was sufficient evidence of proposed misconduct to contact the police and initiate an investigation. Social media has created the potential for making a school administrator's job much more complicated.

Investigations Involving the Department of Social Services

It is imperative that when you suspect one of your students is the subject of either child abuse and/or neglect that you make a report to DSS or its equivalent. I have found that some school administrators are very reticent to make calls to DSS because they believe that angry parents will attempt to retaliate against them in some way. The reality is that some will make threats but you must keep in mind that it is your duty to protect children under your care.

To those who might threaten me, I say "bring it on" because every single child, no matter how "powerful" or "threatening" their parents might be, is worth the call. If one of your staff members, e.g. a. teacher or Guidance Counselor, ever hesitates to contact DSS when there is evidence of abuse or neglect, it is your duty to make the call as the complainant. This is what we are paid for, this is what "real professionals" do.

I once personally called DSS to make a report about a first grader who had two of his front teeth knocked out, allegedly by his father in a fit of anger. The first thing I did was take photographs of the injured student's mouth. I then made the call to DSS and proceeded to leave my office to do classroom observations for a couple of hours. When I returned to my office to check for messages, there was one from the first grader's father, shouting "I'm going to come to school and hammer you von Rohr." My first reaction was to call for a lockdown of the school, next to call the local law enforcement agency about the threat and then personally ensure that all entrances to the school were secured.

The school was 100% secure when the angry parent arrived. As he stood in front of the locked main door to the school facility, the police arrived and shortly thereafter arrested him and took him to the police station. I never saw that parent again. Never play "games" with parents suspected of abusing or neglecting a child, but interact with them both politely and professionally. As long as you act in good faith, you need never apologize for attempting to protect one of your students.

HOW TO OBTAIN INFORMATION

Conducting Interviews and Developing Witnesses Sources

While developing an investigative plan, you should identify as many potential witnesses as possible, most certainly to include the alleged victim of the offense and anyone who could possibly provide the alleged perpetrator with a realistic alibi. My point here is that you need to be 100% impartial, no matter what your personal feelings might be toward any student involved in a reported incident.

Order of Interview

This is one of the most important aspects to conducting a successful investigation in a school setting. The main victim should be interviewed first, followed by any others that have pertinent information about the matter under investigation. Be sure and keep detailed notes as you are conducting interviews. If the investigation is of a really sensitive nature, I will advise the person being interviewed that I will be taking notes since fact-taking becomes a first priority. In my past experience, persons being interviewed will not pay attention to your note-taking as long as you have advised them beforehand you will be doing this. If and when additional witnesses are identified unexpectedly during an interview, they should also be interviewed BEFORE the suspected perpetrator of the offense.

Sequestering Witnesses

Students, being the very social beings they are, do not have the demonstrated ability refrain from talking to their peers if placed within reasonable proximity, so it is imperative to keep them separated while the interview process is in progress. Yes, you can sit them in a Secretary's outer office, but they must not be permitted to speak to one another. An optional technique is to have them come to your room, one by one, from their classroom(s), keeping in mind that once they have been interviewed they do not return to class to discuss and/or reveal the purpose or details about why they were taken out of class in the first place. School Resource Officers (SRO's) can be of great service to you under these conditions and could include keeping witnesses sequestered until your investigation is concluded.

Photo line-ups

If you have a school yearbook and several possible suspects have been named, the use of a photo line-up may be useful. Be sure no names appear on photographs and that when you do a photo line-up all of those whose pictures appear look enough alike so that there is no predetermined prejudice involved.

Reliability of Witnesses

It is important to remember that not all witnesses are of the same quality and that the younger the child, the less reliable their testimony, hence the general legal ruling that children under the age of seven do not yet have the ability to distinguish between right and wrong and/or form real intent. As will be highlighted later, children frequently "lie" about an incident to either protect their reputation or the reputation of their friends and/or peers. How do you determine whether or not a student is telling the truth? One way is to continue to go back over the report in detail to see if their testimony changes. Unless deception is suspected, this does not have to be carried to any extreme, but just enough to satisfy you.

Gaining Student Cooperation

It never hurts to stroke a student's ego, so sometimes by simply remarking "I know you would know about this because you are a very popular student here at _____ and everyone talks to you!" Another phrase that often works with usually well-intended, supportive students is "I know that you are a big part of this school's success and I'm sure you will help me out any way you can to keep the school's reputation good, won't you?"

When You Don't Believe They Are Telling the Truth

When questioning students you believe are lying (you have reliable evidence of this) you might start out with "One thing I won't ask you again is whether or not you know about _____ " or "If you know something and don't tell me, you will be an accessory and can be punished for withholding information." These statements can have different effects on individual students; some will blurt out what they know, others act confused while they assess their position, or, in the case of a "street-wise" student, reaffirm their resolve to say nothing. For the last group, it is doubtful they were ever going to cooperate anyway.

Here are my thoughts on making eye contact while interviewing a student: If you look a student straight into their eyes it could be construed by them as being intimidating, but I do it anyway, in an attempt to determine if they are avoiding eye contact with the issue under investigation. If my initial "gaze" elicits information, I can always change this style to make them feel more comfortable as they divulge information. Remember, this investigative tool is used when you suspect deception; I do not take this direct approach when interviewing a victim. A student or adult witness that turns away from you in their chair, or who starts sweating profusely, should tune you into the thought they are very likely attempting to avoid your questioning.

In regard to "body language," there is, in my opinion, no 100% reliable research that proves that body language can really tell you if a person is telling the truth or not. Keep in mind I said 100%, please read a little between the lines on this. When a student attempts to change the topic of a conversation, don't let them, they are making an active attempt to keep you from asking them direct questions about the matter under investigation.

I strongly recommend that you never lie to a student about who has said what to whom, however, you can always imply, like "what if I told you that Jimmy has told me he saw you put the missing laptop in your locker?" Never make promises you can't keep and be careful if you are bluffing!

Interview Techniques

When does an interview turn into an interrogation? The answer to this is quite simple: when the facts being presented to you by an interviewee are determined to be false or contradictory. If a person reveals information that makes them a suspect, this is the time the course of your conversation changes from interview to interrogation. When a witness suddenly provides information that implicates another student, it is best to maintain a low key demeanor on your part to keep the interviewee both calm and cooperative.

A common technique for eliciting information from a student is to ask them to "help you," which will often initiate the release of information from them when they might otherwise be intimidated by your position as a school administration.

Assessing the Potentially Dangerous Student

There is always the possibility that a student you are interviewing has the potential to harm you, a member of your student body, or a staff member. With this in mind, I highly recommend that school administrators receive training through an organization like "Keys to Safer Schools," located in Bryant, AR. "Keys" offers many courses; to include one that specifically aides school leaders in identifying a potentially dangerous student. Their staff is also available to provide on-site training for deescalating aggressive student behavior. I have used the training I received through "Keys" to successfully identify potentially dangerous students on five actual occasions during my school administration career. On two of those occasions, referral to either law enforcement or mental health professionals quickly followed. No one needs a school shooting to justify the use of this assessment instrument. Please, be proactive when it comes to protecting your charter school students, staff and faculty.

A Review of Some Interview Techniques

"The Lesser of Two Evils"

First, some background. When I served as Quality Control Officer (senior military officer) for the Army's Polygraph program at the U.S. Army Criminal Records Center in Baltimore, Maryland, I had the opportunity to observe my civilian supervisor apply the "Lesser of Two Evils" technique to elicit a confession. A military service member had been accused of shipping a large quantity of hashish through the U.S. diplomatic mail system to the U.S. from Kabul, Afghanistan. After concluding that the soldier was lying, the investigator stared the service member in the eyes and remarked, in a very sincere, deliberate voice, "It is quite obvious you smuggled the drugs, but I am also concerned about whether or not you were are a traitor to your country, collaborating with the Russians. If that's the case, I wouldn't admit that myself; but if it is only the dope smuggling, that is no big deal." These remarks were quickly followed up by "You only smuggled hashish didn't you, you didn't sell out your country, and you're not a traitor, are you?" The soldier's eyes got big as saucers and he shouted, quite emphatically, "No, I am not a traitor, I only tried to smuggle the drugs." That was the day I learned about the "Lesser of Two Evils" interview technique, which can be applied, quite successfully, as an interview tool in a school setting.

How can the "Lesser of Two Evils" technique be utilized by a school administrator? Put into play in a school setting, I once asked a student about one low level theft and then shortly thereafter mentioned that a much more serious one took place in the same timeframe. I commented that taking _____ was one thing, but that taking _____ was much more serious, followed by "If you only took the _____ you might not be in much trouble, but if you stole the _____ that is another thing entirely." Next would be the statement "So, did you just take the_____ (lesser item in value) or did you take both of them? From my experience, the "inexperienced thief" will readily admit to the more minor of the two thefts.

"Bending the Truth"

There are times when it may be useful to "bend the truth" a bit. This is not the same as out and out "lying" and can take the form of "what would you think if I told you Johnny says you _____." As long as you make the comment "what if" you are not stating a fact and, in most cases, students only hear what causes them the most internal conflict, which would be that someone has "tattled" or "snitched" on them. It will be your job to determine how incredulous their response to your statement might be.

Examples of conducting investigations in school settings are included at Appendix N.

CHAPTER 11

Code of Conduct/ Disciplinary Codes

Example: Student Rights, Conduct & Responsibilities

EXPECTATIONS FOR STUDENT CONDUCT AND DISCIPLINE

Rather than offer you personal recommendations as to what you should put in your school's disciplinary code/Code of Conduct, I offer you a sample of the one used at my current school. This offers you the option of using it as it or adapting it to suit your own needs. No school should ever open up without a set of rules/ guidelines for student behavior. If you have to copy it and later change it, so be it, but you will be protected in the meantime. Here is the sample:

_____believes that the goals and objectives for student policies should enhance equal educational opportunity for all students. All procedures and guidelines must be fair, just, and in the best interest of the individual student and the community. Expectations for conduct and discipline are intended to encourage student growth by safeguarding and maintaining an environment conducive to learning as well as to provide public education in an atmosphere where differences are understood and appreciated.

_____will treat all persons fairly, with respect, and without discrimination or threats of violence or abuse. Every student will have equal educational opportunities regardless of ethnic or racial background, religious beliefs, sex, disability, and economic or social conditions. It will be the Principal's responsibility to develop a plan and provide procedures to assure support of the _____ policies regarding student conduct and discipline and to work with the staff and students to ensure equal opportunity for all students in all programs and activities. _____ administrators will periodically review and revise procedures, if necessary, for disciplining students. It is further expected that all procedures will comply with the appropriate state statutes and constitutional provisions and adhere to the discipline procedures provided for in IDEA-Part B, specifically regulating discipline for children with disabilities.

_____procedures regarding student conduct and discipline will emphasize positive behavioral supports to help _____ students develop desirable behaviors as well as eliminate undesirable behaviors. Discipline is a way of teaching and effective teaching is done in a positive manner. Positive means may include: individual discussion and counseling, student involvement in understanding acceptable standards, and parent/legal guardian involvement. All efforts will be made to allow faculty and staff to reinforce positive behaviors and to teach appropriate social skills essential for becoming a well-rounded adult.

As students progress through the school, it is assumed that an increase in age and maturity will require a greater responsibility for actions. Differences in age, maturity and developmental level should be considered when determining the type of disciplinary action and possible intervention needed. Efforts also will be made to address each individual student's unique learning style and developmental level while ensuring a safe and secure learning environment for all students.

All procedures regarding student conduct and discipline will apply to every student as long as the consequences are consistent with the student's IEP, if applicable. If a student's IEP, FBA, or BIP addresses a particular behavior, it generally would be inappropriate to use some other response for the specific behavior(s) identified in the BIP/FBA or IEP. Procedures regarding student conduct and discipline are intended to be applicable to student conduct on and off school premises according to the fullest extent by the law. These times and places include, but are not necessarily limited to, academic programs, field trips, athletic events and school transportation.

Student Expectations

Expectation # 1: All students will obey the law. Any illegal activity occurring during school hours, within the vicinity of the _____ campus, or while participating in any school activity will result in immediate referral to the appropriate law enforcement officials. These activities include, but are not limited to: possession or use of tobacco or alcohol; activities related in any manner to the purchase, use of or distribution of drugs; gang related activities; sexual behavior; possession of weapons or abuse.

Expectation # 2: All students will respect the property of others. Theft, vandalism, inappropriate searches or any other form of mistreatment of property belonging to others, including the school, will result in consequences that may range from an informal conference to out-of-school suspension. It will include restitution of stolen and damaged items or police involvement.

Expectation # 3: All students will respect the ideas, beliefs, cultures and individual differences of others. Students engaged in verbal abuse, intimidation, bullying, cyber bulling, harassment, discrimination, disrespect of authority, fighting, profanity, obscene behavior, extortion, gang-related activities or other such behaviors will receive consequences ranging from informal conference to out-of-school suspension based on severity, prior history and any other factors the administration choose to take into consideration.

Expectation # 4: All students will respect the privilege of education. Tardiness, unexcused absences, plagiarism, cheating, lying, dress code violations, public displays of affection or any form of academic misconduct will result in consequences ranging from an informal conference to out-of-school suspension based on severity, prior history any other factors the administration choose to take into consideration.

DISCIPLINARY ACTIONS

Violations of _____ policies, rules, and regulations will result in disciplinary actions The Board will direct the _____ administration to establish additional rules and regulations necessary to create and preserve conditions essential to orderly operation of the school. The Board will authorize its administrators to employ probation and suspension and to recommend expulsion, if necessary. If there is expulsion with change of placement, Free Appropriate Public Education (FAPE) will be provided.

Corporal Punishment

The use of corporal punishment, defined as any act of physical force upon a student for the purpose of punishing that student, is not acceptable at _____ and will not be tolerated as a disciplinary measure. The school will permit the use of reasonable and necessary physical force under the following circumstances: to quell a disturbance which threatens physical injury to persons, including those students involved, or which threatens serious damage to property; to obtain possession of weapons or other dangerous objects upon the person or within the control of a student; to defend one's self; to remove a student from a classroom or other school property when the student's continued presence poses a threat of danger to other persons or property. To ensure safe and correct handling of students during the situations described above, the Principal or designated staff members will be trained in a prescribed physical restraint method.

Suspension of Students

It is the policy of _____ to provide due process of law to students, parents and school personnel through procedures for the suspension of students which are consistent with federal law, state law and regulation and local policy. Suspension is the exclusion of a student from school and school activities for a period of time not to exceed ten school days for any one offense or ten days in a school year. The Principal may suspend a student from school for commission of any crime, gross immorality, gross misbehavior, persistent disobedience or for violation of written rules and regulations. The Principal may also suspend a student when the presence of the student is detrimental to the best interest of the school. Review of suspension will be discretionary with the Principal. However, the Principal must review suspensions that occur within the last ten days of the school year which would make a student ineligible to receive credit for the school year. The exception to Board approval is if the presence of the student constitutes an actual threat to a class or a school or a hearing is granted within twenty-four hours of the suspension. Whenever a student who is classified as disabled commits a suspendable offense, the Principal or his/her designee will confer with the IAT team before initiating suspension procedures.

The student may appeal the action of the Principal to the _____ Board. The Principal will advise the parent/legal guardian of the right to appeal the Principal's decision to the Board. The parent/legal guardian must give notice of his/her intent to appeal to the Principal, who will promptly, upon receipt of such notice, contact the Board and schedule a date for the appeal. The Board will promptly schedule a parental conference to review the appeal upon request with any parent/ legal guardian. The Board may vacate or revise the Principal's suspension action if he/she believes such action to be appropriate. The Board will inform the parent/legal guardian, either orally at the time of the conference or after the conference in writing of the decision, and provide the Principal with a copy of any written response. Should the Board reject an administrative recommendation for suspension or should a court of final disposition reverse the suspension or expulsion action, the Principal will excuse all student absences resulting from said action.

Expulsion of Students

It is the policy of _____ to provide due process of law to students, parents and school personnel through procedures for the expulsion of students which are consistent with federal law, state law and regulation and local policy. Expulsion is the removal of a student from school for the remainder of the school year or until readmitted by the Principal. Authority to expel students from school rests solely with the Principal. Special education students must still receive FAPE even while expelled from classes on campus.

The following procedures will apply to the expulsion of students. The Principal will notify the parent/legal guardian of the student of the time and place of a hearing to begin expulsion proceedings. At the hearing, the parent/legal guardian will have the right to legal counsel and to all other regular legal rights, including the right to question all witnesses. The hearing will take place within ten days of the written notification at a time and place designated by the Principal, and a decision will be rendered within ten days of the hearing. The student will be suspended from school and all school activities during the time of expulsion procedures, except for scheduled conferences.

The student may appeal the action of the Principal to the   Board. The Principal will advise the parent/legal guardian of the right to appeal the Principal's decision to the Board. The parent/legal guardian must give notice of his/her intent to appeal to the Principal, who will promptly, upon receipt of such notice, contact the Board and schedule a date for the appeal. The Board will promptly schedule a parental conference to review the appeal upon request with any parent/ legal guardian. The Board may vacate or revise the Principal's suspension action if he/ she believes such action to be appropriate. The Board will inform the parent/ legal guardian, either orally at the time of the conference or after the conference in writing of the decision, and provide the Principal with a copy of any written response. Should the   Board reject an administrative recommendation for suspension or should a court of final disposition reverse the suspension or expulsion action, the Principal will excuse all student absences resulting from said action.

Suspension and Expulsion of Students with Disabilities:

School personnel can remove a child with a disability, including suspending or expelling for behavior that is not a manifestation of the child's disability, to the same extent as is done for students without disabilities, for the same behavior.

School personnel can report crimes to appropriate law enforcement and judicial authorities. School personnel can always ask a court for a temporary restraining order in order to protect children or adults from harmful behaviors. _____ policies on suspension and expulsion of students with disabilities will adhere to the specific procedures for disciplinary actions that involve students with disabilities as outlined in IDEA and applicable amendments. The following guidelines will be implemented for compliance thereto.

School personnel can remove a student with a disability for ten consecutive days or less at a time for a violation of the school code of conduct, to the same extent applied to children without disabilities. School personnel can immediately remove for up to ten consecutive schools days or less, the same child for separate incidences of misconduct.

School personnel can also order a change of placement of a child with a disability to an appropriate interim alternative educational setting for up to forty-five days for possession of weapons or drugs or the solicitation or sale of controlled substances while at school and school functions.

If school personnel believe that a child is a danger to himself or others, they can ask a hearing officer in an expedited due process hearing to remove a student to an interim alternative educational setting for up to forty-five days. Forty-five-day interim alternative educational placements can extended be in additional forty-five-day increments if the hearing officer agrees that the child continues to be substantially likely to injure him/her or others if returned to his/her prior educational placement.

Student Absences and Excuses

In accordance with state law, the State Board of Education has established regulations defining lawful and orderly enrollment and attendance of students. The purpose of these regulations is to identify the reasons for the child's continued absence and to develop a plan in conjunction with the student and his/

her parent/legal guardian to improve his/her future attendance. This applies to all students.

School officials will immediately intervene to encourage the student's future attendance when the student has three consecutive unlawful absences or a total of five unlawful absences. The Principal will promptly approve or disapprove any student absences in excess of ten days.

When a student's absence is determined by the Principal or his/her designee to be lawful, the student will be given permission to make-up work missed including tests, reports, homework, etc. The amount of time allowed for make-up will be determined by the teacher for the particular class. If a student's absence is determined by the Principal or his/her designee to be unlawful, there is no obligation on the part of the school personnel for make-up though the student is encouraged to obtain assignments and perform to the best of his/her ability.

Examples of lawful absences include: students who are ill and whose attendance in school would endanger their health or the health of others may be temporarily excused from attendance and students in whose immediate family there is a serious illness or death. Students may be excused from attendance in school for recognized religious holidays of their faith. Students may be excused from attendance in school for the following reasons: doctor, dentist or orthodontist appointment; special family educational trips that have prior approval of the Principal. Trips not acceptable include: hunting trips, recreational trips, attending sporting events as spectator, etc. Students may be excused from attendance in school when they are suspended from school.

Examples of unlawful absences include: students who are willfully absent from school without the knowledge of their parents/legal guardians; students who are absent from school without acceptable cause with the knowledge of their parents/legal guardians; and absences not verified by written permission of parent/legal guardian on the day of return to school after an absence.

It is recognized that many students participate in school sponsored organizations or activities which may lead to absences for school purposes such as competitions, band trips, athletic events, field trips and conventions. While such absences may be for worthwhile causes, they nevertheless result in missed instruction. Activities of this nature must be approved by the Principal. The classroom teacher is responsible for monitoring absences and reporting them to the Principal. Absences will be recorded as unexcused until a proper excuse is recorded with the Principal. It is the Principal's responsibility to notify the classroom teacher of all excused absences.

Intervention for Three [3] Absences: When three consecutive absences or three unlawful absences have accumulated, the teacher will contact parent/legal guardian immediately (phone call, conference, etc.) explaining the attendance policy, encouraging attendance, doctor's excuses, etc. A summary of the conversation will be placed in the student's permanent record. If the parents/ legal guardians cannot be contacted by phone, a letter should be mailed to them with a request that the letter be returned with their signature. If the letter is not returned, document this on a copy of the letter sent to the parents/ legal guardians.

Intervention for Five [5] Absences: Refer the absences to the Principal. Specify the dates and reasons for the absences. The Principal will make a contact through a home visit, phone call, etc., and, together with the IAT will develop a plan with the parent/legal guardian to improve their child's future attendance.

Intervention for Ten [10] Absences: Teacher notifies the Principal in writing of this absence at the time of the daily attendance count. Dates and reasons for absences must be listed. The Principal will make another contact with the parent/ legal guardian and explain the attendance requirements and again, together with IAT revise the plan to improve their child's future attendance.

Beyond Ten Absences: Any absences beyond ten [10], lawful or unlawful, must be approved by the Principal. The Principal must identify the reasons for the child's continued absence and revise the plan in conjunction with the IAT, the student, and his/her parent/legal guardian to improve his/her future attendance. When the student has eleven [11] unlawful absences, notification will be mailed to the parents/legal guardians that the child may be retained in his/her present grade because of an excessive number of unlawful absences. A copy of the letter will be maintained by the Principal. The parents/legal guardians will also be informed that the student must continue to attend school. The family court may be contacted if educational neglect is suspected.

Student Dress

_____ will require that students wear a school uniform to be determined current school administrators. Students who come to school dressed in violation of the dress code will be accompanied to the office and required to make arrangements for other clothing. The Principal may designate school-wide casual days when uniforms will not be required.

Drug and Alcohol Use by Students

No student, regardless of age, will possess, use, sell, purchase, barter, distribute or be under the influence of alcoholic beverages or other controlled substances in the following where an interscholastic athletic contest is taking place); during any field trip; during any trip or activity sponsored by the Board or under the supervision of the Board or its authorized agents. No student will aid, abet, assist or conceal the possession, consumption, purchase or distribution of any alcoholic beverage by any other student or students in any of the circumstances listed above. No student will market or distribute any substance which is represented to be or is substantially similar in color, shape, size or markings of a controlled substance in any of the circumstances listed above. All administrators will cooperate fully with law enforcement agencies and will report to them all information that would be considered pertinent or beneficial in their efforts to stop the sale, possession and use of controlled substances. The administration will, at a minimum, suspend students who violate this policy and refer them to the IAT team, and the administration may seek services from other agencies. Circumstances: on school property (including buildings, grounds, vehicles); at any school-sponsored activity, function or event whether on or off school grounds including any place.

Use, Possession or Distribution of Tobacco Products

It is the policy of _____ to ensure the safety, welfare and health of its students and employees. The use, possession or distribution of any/all tobacco products is determine to stated _____ goals and will result in serious disciplinary consequences on first occurrence. Subsequent incidents of use/possession or distribution of tobacco products may result in long term suspension and/or a recommendation for expulsion.

Weapons in School

It is the policy of _____ to ensure the safety and welfare of its students and employees. The presence of firearms, knives, blackjacks or other weapons on school property poses a severe threat of serious harm or injury to students and staff. While on school grounds, in school buildings, on buses or at school-related functions, students will not possess any item capable of inflicting injury or harm (hereinafter referred to as a weapon) to persons or property when that item is not used in relation to a normal school activity at a scheduled time for the student. No vehicles parked on school property may contain firearms, knives, blackjacks or other items which are generally considered to be weapons.

General Violations

Though not specifically mentioned in this list and levels of violations of behavior, any act which is detrimental to the good order, best interest and physical safety of the school may be punished according to its nature and degree at the discretion of the administration.

_____also recognizes the value of a grievance procedure as a formal method for the resolution of any grievances concerning the treatment of students by school personnel. These grievances may arise from allegations of violations of student legal rights or school policy. In addition, the Board recognizes there may be conditions in the school system that the school could improve and that students should have some means by which they can effectively express their concerns. The school will resolve student complaints and grievances through orderly processes and at the lowest possible level.

A teacher will provide any student or his\her parent/legal guardian the opportunity to discuss a decision or situation that the student considers unjust or unfair. If the incident remains unresolved, the student, his/her parent/legal guardian or the teacher may bring the matter to the Principal's attention for consideration and action. The student may also bring the matter to the attention of class officers or the student council, in grades where such are elected, for possible presentation to the Principal. If the matter is still unresolved, the complaining party may bring it in writing to the Board for review.

Regarding Title IX complaints, students who believe that they have been discriminated against on the basis of their sex have the right to appeal to the Principal. If the student is not satisfied with the decision of the Principal, he/she may appeal to the Board. Regarding Section 504 complaints, students who believe that they have been discriminated against on the basis of their disabling condition have the right to appeal to the Principal. If the student is not satisfied with the decision of the Principal, he/she may appeal to the Board. The Principal will schedule appeals to the Board.

Appeal Process for Student Suspension or Expulsion

An _____ student may appeal to the _____ Board any action of the Principal that results in his/her suspension or expulsion. The student's parent/legal guardian must give written notice of his/her intent to appeal to the Principal, who will promptly, upon receipt of such notice, contact the Board and schedule a date for the appeal. The Board will promptly schedule a parental conference to review the appeal upon request with any parent/ legal guardian. The Board may vacate or revise the Principal's suspension action if he/she believes such action to be appropriate. The Board will inform the parent/legal guardian, either orally at the time of the conference or after the conference in writing of the decision, and provide the Principal with a copy of any written response. Should the _____ Board reject an administrative recommendation for suspension or should a court of final disposition reverse the suspension or expulsion action, the Principal will excuse all student absences resulting from said action.

Explanation of Policies

_____ believes self-discipline is an interpersonal goal of education. Students as well as parents have a responsibility to know and respect the policies, rules and regulations of the school. _____ will notify parents and students regarding the student conduct, rights, and responsibility policies by giving parents and students a copy of the policies, with corresponding explanations, in the student handbook distributed to all students and parents at the beginning of each school year. _____ also will provide an explanation of these policies through orientation sessions held at the school and classroom levels at the beginning of each school year. _____ also will post this information on the _____ website. Parents and students will be required to sign a statement each year that they have read and discussed attendance policies and the complete code of conduct handbook. It is imperative that parents/legal guardians and students realize that these policies apply to all _____ activities and sponsored events both on and off the campus, e.g. during field trips, to the fullest extent permitted by law.

CHAPTER 12

Dress Codes

A school's Dress Code can go a long ways in determining a charter school's success and, as stated in the discussion that follows, you have a lot of choices. It will be your task, based on your personal knowledge of your student demographics, location and intent, to decide how you will handle the issue of "dress code."

Uniforms – Yes or No?

One topic charter schools must invariably address is "Uniforms or Not?" By providing you with some examples from schools where I have served, you will have enough information in hand to make a decision on uniform wear that best fits your own particular charter school. I have seen equal success in charter schools where all students wore strictly enforced uniforms, where no uniforms of any type were worn and where there was a "hybrid" policy on uniform wear. The choice will be yours; however, I will attempt to influence your decision by comparing school environments and what worked.

100% School-Prescribed Dress Code

At my first charter school assignment, at Rocky Mount Prep in Rocky Mount, North Carolina, a strict uniform policy was in effect, requiring boys to wear khaki or navy blue pants and shirts of the same color. Girls were dressed in a similar color scheme, with female clothing choices. The dress code policy has since been changed with the growth of the school from 900 in 2004 to about 1,200 today. Students in the elementary school are currently required to wear navy blue polo shirts with khaki pants, while middle school students wear hunter green polo shirts with khaki pants. High school students wear light blue polo or button-down shirts with khaki pants. School spirit shirts are allowed at designated times. Rocky Mount Prep's free and reduced lunch percentage has remained relatively unchanged, at around 60% (D. Haynes, personal communication, February 8, 2014)

The school's website (rmprep.org/school-uniforms) justifies their rationale for their dress code by stating:

"To help create an environment conducive to learning, all students at Rocky Mount Prep are required to wear uniforms. We believe that students should focus their energy and attention on their academic development and not on style or the clothes of their peers. Dress code is important to school safety since students are often outside of the school facility and students in uniform are easily recognized to all school community members, and research shows it makes a difference with behavior. To ensure that the school's uniform has its desired effect, we require that is it implemented consistently."

What I concluded from the almost five years I served as senior school administrator of what was then North Carolina's largest charter school, was that our "strict" uniform policy definitely worked because was aware of expectations. There was also a significant amount of parental support for uniforms, which made our job as school administrators much easier. When I now look back at my time at this large charter school, I realize that disciplinary problems were few and far between as a result of not having students worry about "who was best dressed" or "who had more money than another." If the issue of income inequality plays as role in your charter school, I contend that uniform wear is an issue that deserves your serious consideration.

The Other Extreme – No Uniforms

On the other end of the continuum of uniform wear is Vance Charter School, where as served as Principal. On the school's website under Frequently Asked Questions, it states "the dress code at Vance Charter School states that students must wear properly fitting clothing. Undergarments must not be visible. Hats are not permitted in the building. Students may not wear clothing with obscene or offensive messages or messages which violate the school's drug-free policy. Students do not wear uniforms at this time." This policy is available at the following website: (www.vancecharter.org/printed/asp?active_page_id=103).

Vance Charter was in the enviable position of being literally the equivalent of the "center of the universe" for offering a truly superior education to public school students in Vance County, one of the poorest in the State of North Carolina. This charter school has flourished since its inception in 1999 due to its high academic achievement. In the four years I was there, they were twice recognized as a "North Carolina Honor School of Excellence" (90%+ on state testing) and twice as a "North Carolina School of Distinction" (80-89% on state testing). In addition, in December of 2007, the State of North Carolina nominated Vance Charter School for recognition in the federal government's "Blue Ribbon Schools" program.

For reasons like this, the school was always filled to its capacity of 500, with a waiting list of an equal number of children. Socioeconomically, the school was not particularly diverse; however, I will note that there were absolutely no policies in place to do anything but encourage anyone from enrolling in the school. Regardless of race, there were no problems with not wearing uniforms, as a result of few in the community being affluent since the textile and tobacco industries went under. Coming from a "uniform" charter school, I wondered if the "no uniform policy" of this school would make a difference, in particular in reference to disciplinary issues. The answer was, after four years of scrutiny, "there was no difference." I do feel the parents of our students at this school appreciated the education their children were receiving so they were especially supportive of our school policy on dress code.

A "Hybrid" Uniform School

Toward the end of the 2010 school year, I received a call from a board member from Spartanburg Charter School, which I found out was located right in the downtown center of Spartanburg, South Carolina. Since I had long since given my notice at Vance Charter School (four years in a town of only 18,000 was enough for me) and I had, during my military career, two very productive assignments in South Carolina, I let the board member know I was definitely interested. I reviewed the school's website and quickly noted that this was a start-up charter school, one that opened eight months earlier in August of 2009. Within a week, I visited the school and noted that they utilized what I would characterize as a "hybrid" uniform policy. Boys at this school wore khaki or navy blue pants and navy blue, kelly green or brown generic polo shirts. Girls wore Pants and/or dresses in either khaki or navy blue and polo shirts in the school colors: navy blue, kelly green or brown. Over the past four plus years, I have "loosened my grip" a bit and allow the wearing of our "official" Friday shirts, which represent student participation in school clubs, sports, or the ones we give, free, to every student each year to celebrate our school's latest accomplishment. Our most recent version notes our designation as a "National Blue Ribbon Lighthouse School of Excellence."

On April 15th of each school year, the "shirts tucked in" policy is extinguished for the remainder of the school year. (Note: grades K-3 may wear their shirts out all year 'round). With this dress code and a truly wonderful group of students here at Spartanburg Prep, I have had few serious disciplinary problems. Note: the polo shirts our students wear are generic in nature and can be purchased at several retail outlets in the local area. We eventually devised a "wear out policy" (one year) for the old school colors of kelly green and brown as we moved on to the student-chosen colors of navy blue and light blue (note: never call it "Carolina Blue" in South Carolina!).

As a parting note on this topic, the school picks up the tab for all assigned staff for one navy blue polo shirt per year and encourages them to wear that shirt on

Mondays (when weather permits). There is a great deal of latitude given to staff members in regard to their choice of color for the staff polo and with the many Clemson and South Carolina graduates on our staff it is not unusual to see lots of garnet and orange in the building. As long the polo shirt contains the same information as the school purchased polo shirts, e.g. "Spartanburg Prep School" on the left side of the chest, there is no problem. Students have not made any objections to staff wearing colors they can't wear, they acknowledge that adults have privileges.

CHAPTER 13

School Security

School safety is an area that must be addressed when either starting up a charter school or successfully operating one. Even before the tragedy in Newtown, Connecticut, I attended every school safety seminar offered in this state, with a certificate noting my training hanging on the wall in my school office. Keep in mind that even though I have over twenty years of law enforcement experience and the fact I was once nationally certified in educational security, I continue to engage in professional development pertaining to school security.

The charter school I currently serve at has been rated as "very secure" by both local and state law enforcement agencies and we want to keep it that way. You need to start out by having the proper daily operational plans for a crisis (See Appendix K as an example). A school safety plan known only by the Principal and his administrative staff will not be a successful one. All of the teaching and administrative staff must be familiar with it, not only on paper, but in real life, practical application. In other words, they need to participate in crisis management drills, just the same as you do for fires, tornadoes, hurricanes or any other natural disaster your routinely prep for. "Lockdown drills," where every classroom is secured, with children out of sight of anyone looking into the room, need to be conducted, and recorded on record, several times each school year. I also recommend conducting an annual school-wide "relocation drill," at which time all of your students relocate to a secure facility near your campus. Be sure and document these drills!

Public Address System

There are many reasons to have a public address system in your school, the most important being school security. When you are able to successfully pass on information, immediately, to everyone in the school, you are proactive. Without the presence of a school-wide communication device, you are seriously reducing your school's security posture. The cost of installing such a system can be measured in reduced liability for your school. The cost for installation of a public address system at our school and the ability for teachers to "push a button" and reach the school office was about $9,000.00 at my current school.

One question frequently asked is what to call these drills and how to announce them over your school's public address system? My preference is for colors to designate things that need attention in the building like "vomit" clean-up in the hallway (Code Green) or Code Red for missing students.

When it becomes necessary to alert staff to imminent danger, we use letter codes, for example:

Code __ (Your chosen alphabetic letter goes here) : This code signifies there is an event taking place where all students and staff need to proceed with caution, i.e. a student is contained but showing violent behavior; a person who has been pulled over by the police in your immediate area and has fled on foot, etc. At this time all students are to be secured in their classrooms; bathrooms and hallways are to be cleared by staff, with students relocated to their homeroom; while in the same time frame teachers are to calmly walk to their classroom door and lock it. No one is to leave their classroom at any time until an "All Clear" is heard throughout the building. Staff should continue teaching when this code is in effect.

Campus Entry

Whether already in place or in the process of design, I highly recommend your school has the ability to view and challenge a person about their reason to enter your school facility before they are allowed in. This requires a camera and a microphone on the outside door. Once a person is "buzzed in," they should be going straight into the school's office. Once in our school office, they must sign in on a visitor's roster, produce their driver's license and then scan it on our screening machine to ascertain whether or not they have a criminal record. With the system we now have in place, should a criminal offender be identified, a text message is immediately sent to both the Principal and Assistant Principal. If there is no problem with the driver's license scan, the person is issued a label, printed out on the scanner device. The individual will only be allowed to leave the office area once they have their office label on, which has their photo on it. Before exiting the school, visitors must be buzzed into the office door and sign out before finally departing.

Another level of school security to give consideration to is a "panic button" under the receptionist's desk. When such a device is in use, police receive notification just like a 911 call, in this case noting an emergency at a public school. It is imperative to test this type of system several times during the school year. Be sure to notify the local law enforcement agency when you are just testing the system for response time.

We have figured out that no matter how quickly law enforcement can respond to our school, if they are not familiar with the school's physical layout they are at a serious disadvantage. In the proactive mode, we have coordinated with representatives of both our local law enforcement agencies (Spartanburg Police and Sheriff's Office), with the result that they not only have copies of our floor plans but have taken tours of our school facility. Everyone on our staff has received training about what their part is in a crisis situation, to include one involving an "active shooter" scenario.

Surveillance Cameras

For the past two years, we have had surveillance cameras (8) at the back of our school to enable us to monitor the elementary playground, the sides of the school from front to back and the outdoor basketball court. We have had numerous incidents reported that were sorted out through playback on the DVR. One of the benefits of the use of the surveillance cameras is to prove to parents that their child did in fact engage in some inappropriate physical event while outside. The old "My child would not do that" became a thing of the past once video surveillance of the playground area was initiated. The start-up cost for installation of eight surveillance cameras at the back of our school in 2011 was $12,000.00.

It is our intent to add additional, higher definition cameras so that we are able to more successfully monitor both recess activity and children participating in our after school program.

More Security Alerts in a School Setting

Code__ (Your chosen alphabetic letter goes here): This code is used when there is an event taking place that IS NOT under control, e.g. someone has entered the building who is unwanted and who is at high risk of causing harm to students and/or staff. When this code goes into effort, everyone is asked to move quickly and calmly while gathering students from the hallway and bathrooms as if the unwanted person is already on the move through the building. Once a teacher has all of their students locked inside their classrooms, they are to: (1) Turn out the lights in their classroom; (2) Have students gather at the back of the room in the corner on the same wall as the door opening to the hallway and get on the floor with their knees facing the wall, very quietly. For example, in Ms. "Jones' room," students would gather in the corner of the room where her desk is. This strategic relocation of students is made with the intent of giving any person we are trying to avoid the impression that our classrooms are empty when they look into them from the glass section of the classroom doorways. Teachers are asked to keep their students as quiet and calm as possible, with a decided effort to avoid any kind of panic. This student "mentality" only exhibits itself after you have conducted lockdown drills several times. No one is to leave their secured area until an ALL CLEAR is heard throughout the building.

School Resource Officer (SRO)

When it comes to school safety, the presence of an SRO will inevitably come up as a topic of discussion. My recommendation: If you have the funds to support the hiring of an SRO, do it. At my first charter school, with close to 1,000 students, we had two RSO's in the building, one assigned to the elementary school, the second in the middle/high school wing school on the other side of the campus. These were private security officers on our payroll since the country Sheriff's Office wanted to charge us more money that we could afford.

For years, my current charter school board of directors had been discussing the issue of hiring a SRO. With the occurrence of the incident at Newtown and subsequent incidents of school violence, it was time to take another look at our security posture. In the Fall of 2013, the school applied for a federal grant for an SRO through the local Sheriff's Office. In January of 2014, we were advised that although initially approved we would not be a recipient of any funding, at which time my Board of Directors, made up primarily of parent members, approved the hiring of Sheriff's Deputies on a part-time basis. Since the cost for one, full-time Deputy was $59,000 per year, versus $36,000 per year using part-time personnel, hiring part-timers was their decision. Financial considerations must always come into consideration when operating a charter school, but we accomplished just what we wanted, to improve our already high level of school security in place.

CHAPTER 14

The Issue of Retention

As a public school administrator, the issue of student retention is bound to come up. How you manage this matter will reflect upon your professionalism; do it right and you will have a very positive relationship with parents; do it wrong and your reputation may/will suffer accordingly.

In a traditional school setting, decisions on retention most often come about as a result of subjective discussions among school personnel, with school administrators taking into consideration teacher input, followed by a formal recommendation.

If this process sounds familiar, don't feel bad, because it is the same way I made retention decisions for quite some time; however, for the past eight I have used a much more objective process to help me come to a decision about a student's suitability for promotion to a higher grade. The difference in meeting a parent, with only opinion, versus objective data in hand, should not be underestimated.

Light's Retention Scale (Academic Therapy Solutions, 2006) can be a virtual lifesaver when it comes to assisting you in making decisions about retentions. This assessment instrument covers twenty separate factors in a student's life, to include the following:

Pre-School Attendance, Current Grade Placement, Age of Student, Physical Size, The Sex of Students and Grade Progress, Previous Grade Retention, The Student's Knowledge of the English Language, Immature Behavior, Emotional Disorders, History of Problems with Conduct or Behavior, Experiences in the Life of the Child, Siblings, Parent Participation in School Activities, Family Moves (Student Mobility), School Attendance, Current Level of Academic Achievement, Attitude of the Student About Possible Retention, Motivation for Finishing Their Homework, History of Learning Disabilities and Estimate of Student's Intelligence.

In addition to having this assessment instrument at the school administrator's disposal, a Parent's Guide to Retention accompanies the rating scale, with the purpose of explaining to parents just how retention decisions are made through the use of objective data, not simply in the court of personal opinion.

I also recommend the mention of Light's Retention Scale when you first to speak to parents about the possibility of retention for the following school year. I strongly recommend that you do not wait longer than February to formally address this issue. The difference between using only personal/professional opinion or judgment to make retention decisions, versus a combination of professional opinion and an objective assessment instrument is significant.

CHAPTER 15

Communicating with Parents

If you don't effectively communicate with parents, your job in-place may be fleeting. As a charter school leader, board member, or board of directors, your most important job will be to effectively communicate with your stakeholders, who are primarily composed of parents. Effective communication can take many forms, whether it is accomplished through written correspondence such as monthly newsletters or weekly emails sent home to parents (i.e. Spartanburg Prep emails parents a weekly version of "What's New at Spartanburg Prep?"). This does not imply that this method is 100% effective; individual parent concerns about school issues must be addressed "old school style" via telephone calls. There can be a real danger relying only on email to communicate, with parents in particular. I am not making this comment from my perspective as a "baby boomer," but from a recognition that while times have changed, effective communication may not have caught up with 2014 when it comes to people (parents?) making their own interpretation about what you are "actually" inferring in your emails.

I propose that there are going to be times (no one will be free from this scrutiny) when parents will come to their own personal interpretation about what you "meant" in your email. When you receive an "aggressive" response from a parent, when you thought what you said was quite polite, you have identified a "communication problem." From my own practical experience, I have come to the conclusion that the only way to remedy this situation is to pick up the telephone and apologize to the recipient of the email for any misunderstanding.

Keeping this guidance in mind, I highly recommend the "less is more" philosophy be put into place when it comes to communicating with parents, meaning that you need to keep all of your emails to parents succinct, quite to the point(s) and not going on and on trying to make your point. This is the same "KISS" (keep it simple stupid) guidance I have heard from every one of my educational superiors.

Now, let's talk about administrator/parent interaction. I have traditionally made it a point to be out in front of my school building in the morning to open car doors as parents drop off their children. Being out there in front is always my first intent and I make it a "von Rohr standard," when I am there, to wave at each and every car that goes through the line. I admit I gain personal pleasure in seeing parents wave back at me, even if I am not the one who opened their car door.

Another strategy of "personalization" is to sit in the lobby as students walk into the one entrance into our school in the morning. I do my best to ensure that I say something to every one of them, whether it be "Good Morning Susie," (just an example, all of my students are not named "Susie"), "How are you this morning?" or "Are you ready for school today?" I sometimes reverse this practice and sit just inside the doors where students exit the building at the end of the day and ask value questions like "Did you have a good day today at school?" At other times, I make remarks like "See you tomorrow" so they know that I think of them as individuals, not numbers. Indeed, this is all common sense, but it is things like this that separate a "popular" Principal from the one who is "isolated" from students and their parents. Think about it, how often did your school leaders ever address you directly? Why not more? Because no one ever told them it was important. Although I am no longer 6'5" and 270lbs., and have long-forgotten being muscular ever again, I am still "big' enough to be a physical presence at my school. These are "my" children for almost eight hours every day, so I want to have a non-threatening relationship with them. Mutual respect is my goal. I do recognize that as a charter school becomes larger, it is much more difficult to establish a "benevolent" presence as school leader.

When I went back to Rocky Mount Prep for a middle school basketball game after being gone from that school for four years, students come up to me and asked

"Are you coming back?" I felt really, really good, recognizing that I did something right when it came to communicating with students while I served there.

I will never claim that communication cannot be improved at every possible level; my philosophy here is that you need to figure out how your parents feel about your information exchange with them, and then do everything you can to improve it!

For board members, it is important to ensure that parents are aware of board meeting times and date. I propose that if they attend even once they will see what a tough, often tedious job you have, one you are not receiving a penny for. Be prepared if you have an "open forum" for parents, that is one time you may find yourself with a grimace on your face while they provide their opinion about how someone is not doing their job to their satisfaction. Parents who come to speak during "parent comment time" may keep returning if you give undue credence to their sometimes irrational complaints. Hopefully, true concerns will have been addressed by your lead school administrator before it is brought to your attention as board members.

There are a wide variety of devices available to schools to improve parent-school communication, among them the one we have used at my past two schools, called Blackboard Connect (www.blackboard.com). Some states provide state-wide public school "platforms" for keeping parents in contact with what is going on at schools, to include some who provide parents with access to the daily recording of grades, like South Carolina's "Powerschool." Although I believe we keep our parents up-to-date with weekly emails, notices of a "must know" nature, such as school closings due to inclement weather, need to go out immediately, to some media source.

Whether it is parents or other stakeholders, it is the duty of the leader of the school and the board of directors to keep parents informed about what is going on in the school in a timely and informative manner.

CHAPTER 16

Advertising/Marketing

There are numerous ways to advertise and /or market your school to the public. In the span of sixteen years in leading charter schools, I've probably tried them all, to include putting ads in local and regional parent magazines; in newspapers; advertising at movie theatres; holding "play dates" at local parks to generate initial interest in the school; hosting Open Houses at the school and advertising on billboards located in the community. In our latest marketing effort, we have a full page ad in our local Chamber of Commerce's interactive map.

What/Who is the most successful vehicle for ensuring great public relations for your school? The answer is, undoubtedly, "word of mouth." When you have satisfied parents, they will recruit for you, most likely the same kind of highly motivated parents you already have in your charter school. It is always a good idea to have a place on your student application so parents can comment about how they heard about your school. This information will provide you with the data you need to direct your advertising efforts it the future. Stated once more, money can't buy the best advertising aide you already have on hand; those parents who continue to make your charter school their school of choice. Some schools have promoted "contests" to see which of their families can recruit the most students into the school. My opinion on this is simple, if it works, do it!

CHAPTER 17

School Lunch Programs

Your lunch program options as a charter school are going to be dictated by your school facility. At Rocky Mount Prep, we initially used a local vendor to provide lunch while we were part of the United States Department of Agriculture (USDA) lunch program. When we moved into the permanent school facility in 2001, we continued to be part of the USDA lunch program and used a national level vendor who was headquartered across the street at a private four-year college. The meals were prepared at the college and then transported by vehicle to the school while they were still hot. By 2003, with the addition of the high school wing, a separate cafeteria was set up for high school students. The food in the high school cafeteria was cooked at the facility across the street and then transferred to our school, where it was kept hot in heating devices until being served.

Many other charter schools, like the one I led in Greensboro, North Carolina, also used vendors in order to be able to serve hot lunches to their students and remain part of the USDA lunch program. It is of paramount importance to ensure that the individual who heads up your school's USDA lunch program is proficient at doing the required paperwork which can be very time-consuming.

Many charter schools in the United States are not part of the USDA lunch program and have therefore had to come up with other ideas for lunch. Some simply have their students bring their own lunch to school, or have days when specific types of food (e.g. pizza, tacos, and chicken sandwiches) are brought in by local fast food vendors.

When I arrived at my current school, the lunch offerings were pitiful, keeping in mind that the school was then, in 2010, only receiving only $2,300 per student, per year, in funding. Our state-wide authority, the South Carolina Public Charter School District, ranked 50th in the United States in per pupil student funding. The school was, literally, "dirt poor" since the budget did not have any funding to expand the lunch program. The school was not part of the USDA lunch program. One of my first questions when arriving in March of 2010 was "why not?"

We pursued several companies about contracts to provide our students with a healthy, nutritious lunch and finally found a willing partnership with Preferred Meals (www.preferredmeals.com) a national school food service company located in Berkeley, IL. It is not my intent to promote one company or another, but I will comment that no other food service company was willing to work with a school as small as ours was at the time (300 students). Preferred Meals supplied all of the needed refrigeration, heating devices and other equipment that would allow my school to meet USDA requirements. Under this program, pre-prepared entrees are heated to prescribed temperatures in ovens; milk is kept in refrigeration devices; and fresh fruit and vegetables are delivered almost daily by mostly local vendors chosen by Preferred Meals. We have been part of the USDA lunch program for four years now and have never regretted making the decision to take that extra step. Our students are now the recipients of healthy, nutritious meals on a daily basis. Of course, students who qualify for Free or Reduced Lunch benefit greatly from having the USDA program available to them, otherwise their nutritional needs might not be met. The USDA program is nothing to fear and I sincerely believe that its benefits far outweigh any possible negatives associated with the paperwork requirements.

CHAPTER 18

Grant Writing

Grant writing is indeed an interesting topic! I am going to be completely honest with you're here, I find it incredibly difficult to write grants while running a charter school. However, when you are in crisis like I was in 1999, after the destruction of my charter school in Rocky Mount, NC you have no choice but to get actively involved in any possible fund raising. In that situation, after two members of my Board of Directors failed to get FEMA to support construction of a new school, I intervened, gave my personal perspective to FEMA representative about how we deserved government support and walked away from a luncheon meeting with a $4.6 million dollar grant. Yes, $4.6 million of the cost of the new school (which cost about $8 million) was paid for by a FEMA grant. The federal government came through! After spending six months after the destruction of my school at churches and another fifteen months in portables, we were getting a new, built from the ground up school to open on a 32 acre campus adjacent to a four year private college.

During the period 2004-2010, the schools I worked at hired outside people to do their grant writing, with no discernible results.

In 2010, when my current charter school was suffering a deep financial crisis, help came in the form of Joan Lange, National Schools Director for the Challenge Foundation. After paying a visit to my school and being impressed with our staff and overall efforts to provide an education to a very diverse student population, she rewarded us with an outright grant of $50,000 to help us pay our operational expenses. I still have a copy of my photograph on my wall of Joan handing me the check. Charter schools can never have enough friends.

My recommendation: If you have a good case for obtaining a grant, writing a proposal is never a bad idea. Many of my teachers write "teacher grants," usually for amounts of $3,000 or less and they are frequently rewarded for their efforts. I am, of course, aware of organizations that will write grant proposals for you for a percentage of the total grant award. Honestly, I would only take this option if I felt very confident about our chances to be awarded a grant and that it was legal to pay a grant writing fee. I have at times become frustrated when I have seen traditional public schools awarded grants and/or rewards when I did not feel they were anywhere near as deserving as the charter school where I served. Unfortunately, as charter schools we still have a long way to go to improve our image in the public eye. I do not believe this phenomenon exists because we are not doing a great job; only that all the hard work we put in is often regulated to "second page news" by many media sources, most of whom have no idea what a "charter school" really is. All we can do is our best to become known for what we stand for.

APPENDIX A

New Construction

Rocky Mount Preparatory Charter School, located in Rocky Mount, NC, currently serves about 1,200 students in grades K5-12 in a 110,000 square school facility (D. Haynes, personal communication, February 8, 2014). When the school opened in 2001, the campus consisted of about 70,000 square feet. The high school wing and gymnasium were completed in 2004, adding another 32,000 square feet, two years later an additional academic wing of approximately 8,000 square feet of classroom space was built to accommodate an increase in student population.

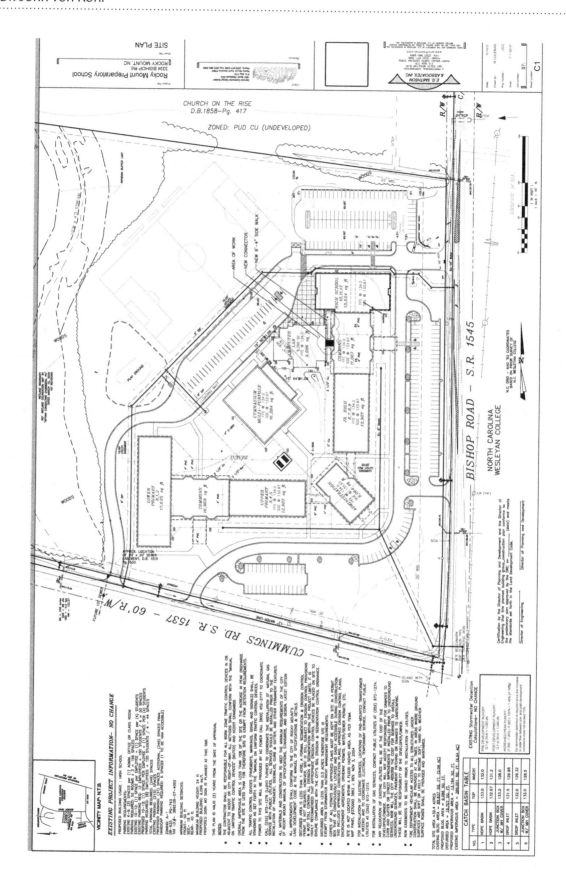

APPENDIX B

Photos of Rocky Mount Prep

Photo of Entrance to Main Administrative Building (2004, Above)

Rear of High School Wing (2004)

Photo of Middle School Hallway (2004)

APPENDIX C

Certificate of Achievement

Certificate of Achievement

Presented to

John von Rohr

Be it known that the Board of Directors of the Rocky Mount Charter School, on behalf of parents and students, commends the faculty and staff of the 1999-2000 school year and awards them this Certificate of Achievement.

- For their outstanding services and enduring patience in re-locating the school twice after being flooded out by Hurricane Floyd;

- For their ingenuity in: managing operations at three locations; congested classrooms, offices and hallways; and restless students;

- For completing a difficult year with professionalism, dignity, good humor, and sanity intact.

For the Board:

Robert R. Mauldin, Chairman

June 8, 2000

Spartanburg Preparatory School Original Plans for School Facility

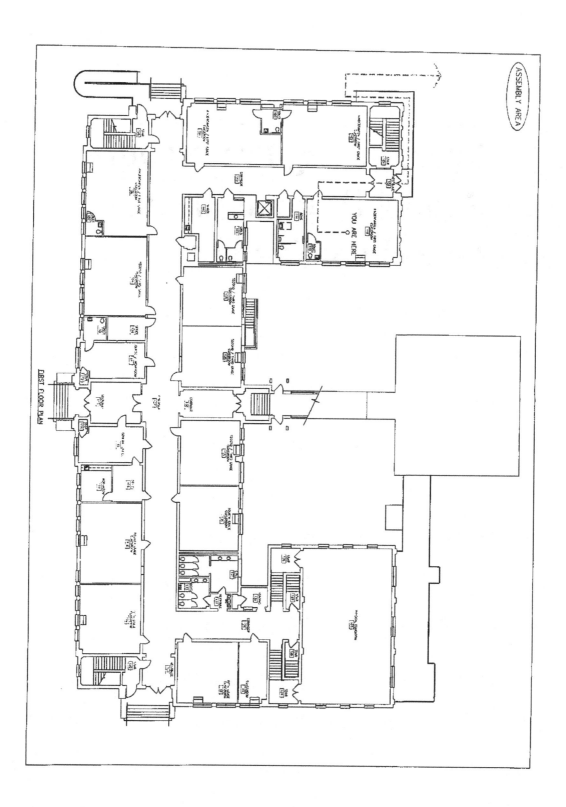

FIRST FLOOR PLAN

ASSEMBLY AREA

YOU ARE HERE

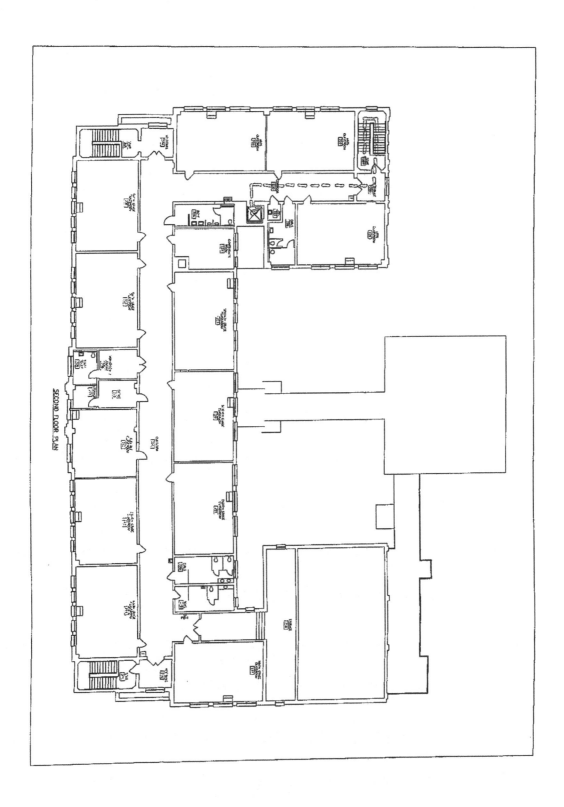

APPENDIX E

Green Charter School (2014)

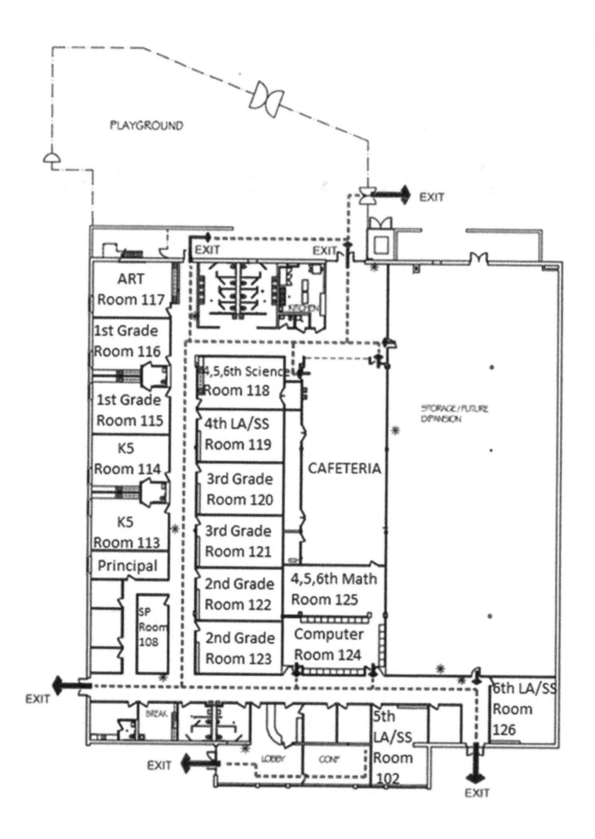

Examples of Renovated Facilities Integrity Real Estate Developers

Front View of North Main Academy, Columbia, SC

$2.5 Million Renovation

Rear View of North Main Academy

Orangeburg Charter for Health Professions,
Orangeburg, SC
$2.8 Million Renovation

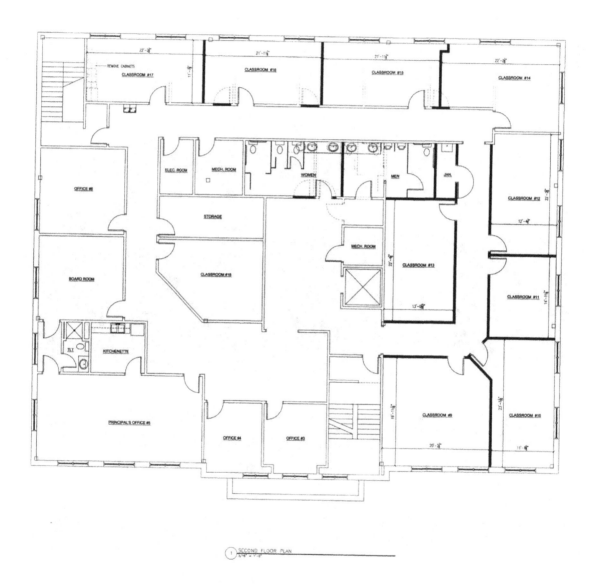

First Floor Plans

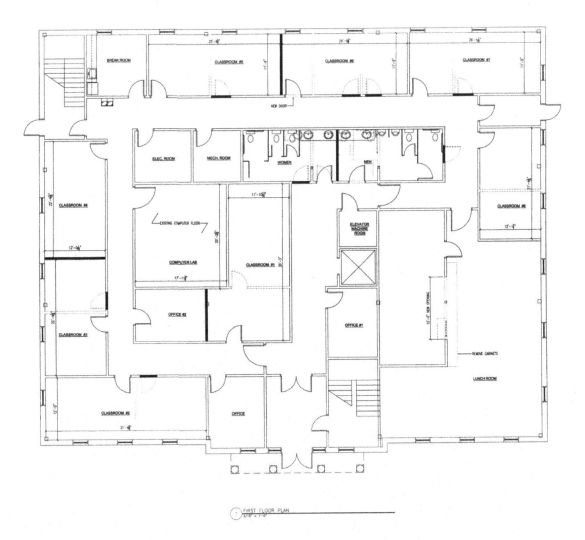

Second Floor Plans

Example of a Modular Royal Live Oaks Academy Vanguard Modular

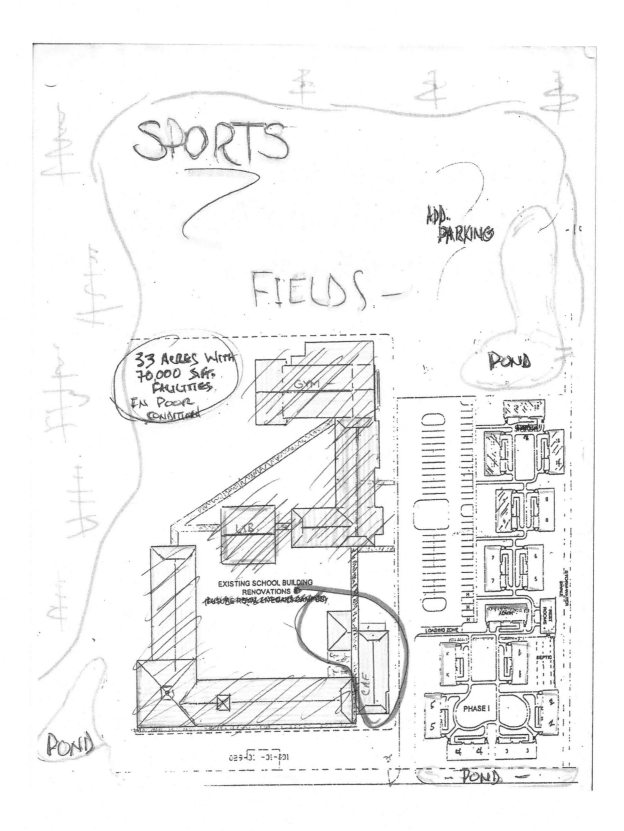

Modular Charter School Campus Plans Vanguard Modular

HOME   ABOUT   WHY MODULAR?   MODULAR SOLUTIONS   SERVICES   GET A QUOTE   CONTACT US

MODULAR SOLUTIONS

- Why Modular?
- Temporary vs. Permanent
- Temporary Modular Solutions
- Permanent Modular Solutions
- Custom Modular Design
- Used Modular Buildings
- Green Buildings
- Financing
- Safe Construction

Modular Solutions

Modular buildings provide additional space solutions you need when you need it within budget and in a compressed schedule. We offer custom-designed floor plans, standard modular building floor plans, and a list of many ancilary site services combined with competive prices to make sure you get what you need without paying too much!

We encourage you to explore the unique benefits of temporary modular construction and of permanent modular buildings. Be sure to take a look at all we can do for you in the area of Custom Modular Design. The exact modular building floor plan you need is just a phone call away! Dial 1-877-438-8627 to reach your friendly local sales representative.

We offer both Temporary Modular Buildings and Permanent Modular Construction for every type of space need, including:

- **Commercial & Retail** (temporary | permanent)
- **Education** (temporary | permanent)
- **Healthcare & Medical** (temporary | permanent)
- **Government** (temporary | permanent)
- **Industrial, Energy, & Utility** (temporary | permanent)
- **Worship** (temporary | permanent)
- **Disaster Recovery** (temporary | permanent)
- **Corrections** (permanent)

Modular building floor plans are completely versatile: perfect for every industry, business, and organization.

BIG SAVINGS!

Check out our fleet of low cost used modular buildings available for immediate delivery!

To request a quote or more information, fill out our Quote Request Form, or simply call us at 1-877-438-8627 today!

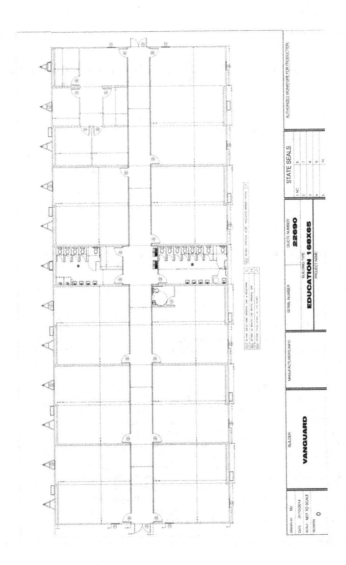

VANGUARD
MODULAR BUILDING SYSTEMS
www.vanguardmodular.com

Modular Project Description

The information provided in this budgetary estimate is prepared for the referenced organization and is CONFIDENTIAL. Unauthorized distribution of this information is strictly prohibited.

Prepared For: **Sample Idea for S.C. Public Educational Use**	Estimate Date: **March 1, 2014**
Project No: **168'x65' CLS**	Revision No:

Building Features:

(1) 168'x65' NEW S.C. Educational Coded Building
(Building #: Building to be built NEW-Serial # to be announced)

(1) Base Building Purchase Price: ~$390,500.00

(2) Operating Lease:
3 Year Operating Lease- ~$9,135.00/month
4 Year Operating Lease- ~$8,545.00/month
5 Year Operating Lease- ~$7,950.00/month

(3) Finance Lease Options: *(Own building at end of payments for $1.00)*
5 Year Finance Lease - ~$7,535.00/month
6 Year Finance Lease - ~$6,670.00/month
7 Year Finance Lease - ~$5,930.00/month

Delivery Set-up, Removal and Other Services provided:
Below is an estimate of Installation Charges and Options:

(**Options available to "roll in" these charges into the Monthly Lease payments, pending credit approval.**)

Transportation of Building	No Charge if ordered before April 15th
Dug and Poured Concrete Footings per Blue Prints	~$23,500.00
Surewall Bonding Agent applied to Block under Building	~$5,900.00
Set-Up/Erection (standard block, level, anchor, and seam)	~$30,000.00
VINYL Skirting/Underpinning	~$3,500.00

Project Assumptions-But not Limited to:
Quoted on level, flat, accessible dirt surface (3,000 psf), not to exceed 6" slope within 100'.
Set-Up is proposed as: Standard double dry stack CMU piers 8' on center and anchors in dry soil
Typical Set-Up floor height of buildings vary depending on building used, but shall not be higher than 40" from ground to bottom of door seal at highest point due to customer site. Additional charges may apply.
If anchors different than dirt anchors needed, additional charges accordingly.
All buildings are quoted to Seismic C Zone, unless otherwise stated.
If digging footings, no removal of dirt is quoted above. It will be left under the building.
Customer is responsible for locating **any and all** underground utilities before work begins.
Plastic/Poly/Vapor Barrier ground coverings are not included in above pricing
If building can not be properly spotted on-site with standard truck, **spotting fees will be incurred.**
All quotes are contingent upon Vanguard Corporate Offices approvals. (Quote has not been submitted).
Dismantle and return charges are quoted at time building is returned.
Pricing does not include and sales, property, or use taxes.
Permits, utility connections, infrastructure, and any site work to be done by others, unless agreed upon.

APPENDIX I

Soldier Hollow Modular Campus Williams-Scotsman

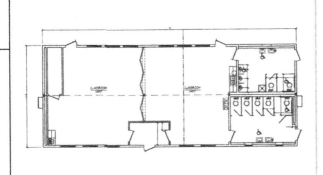

Solider Hollow Charter School
Midway, Utah

The Williams Scotsman Solution

Originally on a fast track for completion in the fall of 2009, the project was delayed several months due to unanticipated code reviews, countless modifications to the agreed upon design and materials, as well as inclement weather. Despite all these challenges, Williams Scotsman consistently met the client's needs in a timely and professional manner to deliver the project within budget and in line with the constantly shifting schedule and milestones.

The Result

Over 6,000 square feet of portable modular classroom space was created with 70'x15' composite decks to allow for outdoor dining, event observation, and expanded classroom environments. Williams Scotsman provided multi-use buildings – classrooms, school assembly rooms, public sporting event observation centers – that incorporated environmentally-friendly design elements to enhance the space. The buildings' interior features include warm tones, ample windows, and vaulted ceilings with clear story windows to create openness and complement the schools focus on the environment and outdoor learning.

"I would unequivocally recommend Williams Scotsman to others interested in undertaking a challenging custom project such as ours!"

– Kimberly Gilboy, EdD
Project Manager, Board Treasurer

DATE ORDER
WAS RECEIVED:
1/13/10

DATE OF DELIVERY:
6/7/10

DATE OF
INSTALLATION/
COMPLETION:
8/13/10

MWRCS-0811-8M © Williams Scotsman 2011

GRIFFITHSVILLE ELEMENTARY SCHOOL

LINCOLN COUNTY BOARD OF EDUCATION
GRIFFITHSVILLE ELEMENTARY SCHOOL
Griffithsville, West Virginia

Client Project

When a flood destroyed Griffithsville Elementary School in West Virginia, students, teachers, and administrative staff were displaced. The Lincoln County Board of Education had to find a quick solution in order to minimize any disruption to the school year. The initial solution placed the elementary school students in the same building and classrooms that were being occupied by the students at the nearby high school. Sharing classroom space and combining the age groups were not efficient solutions since they did not create an optimum learning environment and, displeased parents.

Client Need

The flood created two challenges for the school and the Board of Education. First, the elementary school students needed immediate space so classes could resume as normal. Since school was in session, timeliness was a major factor. Secondly, since FEMA funded the reconstruction project, site plans had to remain flexible to work around the historic house already located on campus. The Lincoln County Board of Education decided that the school required a construction solution that was both flexible and fast.

LINCOLN COUNTY BOARD OF EDUCATION
GRIFFITHSVILLE ELEMENTARY SCHOOL
Griffithsville, West Virginia

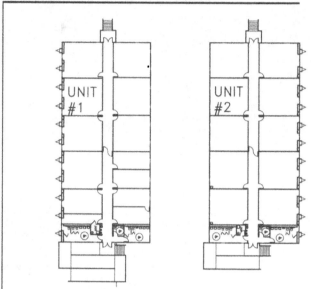

The Williams Scotsman Solution

Williams Scotsman provided the school with temporary classrooms within a month of the permit issue date. Two-11 piece Redi-Plex complexes were installed. Each Redi-Plex unit afforded 7,920 sq. feet. of new space to the school. The building had a drop ceiling, VCG interior walls, vinyl tile flooring, and a Dura-Temp exterior. Williams Scotsman designed restrooms specifically for use by small school children. J-boxes were installed to house a fire alarm system and data cabling for classrooms. Lastly, Williams Scotsman installed anchors and footers, and completed the exterior of the building with steps, ramps, and skirting.

The Result

The Lincoln County Board of Education was fully satisfied with the buildings and the quick, friendly service they received from Williams Scotsman and looking forward to working with them again in the future, if needed.

"Under the adverse site conditions, we are very pleased with the timeframe it took to complete the project. They completed the project with speed and efficiency as promised. Williams Scotsman did very well and we thank them." -David Vickers, Head of Maintenance-

APPENDIX J

Sample Teacher Contract

School Letterhead Paper

Date

Teachers Name

Street Address

City, State, Zip Code

Dear _____

On behalf of _____, I am pleased to offer you the following teaching position for the 2014-2015 school year: Third Grade Teacher.

In accepting this position, you acknowledge that you possess the professional qualifications prerequisite to this position (a valid, current South Carolina teaching certificate, if required) and that failure to maintain these qualifications during the agreement period shall automatically terminate this agreement.

This agreement is subject to all duties prescribed by the laws of the State of South Carolina and any concomitant administrative rules and regulations. In addition, you agree to render services acceptable to the administration, and to faithfully discharge such duties as may be reasonably prescribed by th e _____ administration or its designated representatives. It is understood that you will cooperate with the administration and faculty to promote the _____ mission. Failure to conform to any part of this agreement will constitute sufficient cause to terminate the agreement at will.

In consideration of this agreement, the _____ agrees to pay you for professional services during the agreement period in the amount of $_____ and any loss or reduction in any amount of this funding shall, at the discretion of _____, result in the termination of this agreement or the reduction of the payments to be made for the services under this agreement.

Please acknowledge your acceptance of the terms and conditions of this agreement and your intent to serve in this position during the upcoming school year by signing below. By so signing, you acknowledge that your acceptance will not breach or otherwise violate any other contract with another employer. Furthermore, that your teaching license may be subject to revocation should you sign this contract and then obtain employment in another public school setting in South Carolina.

_____ does not offer tenured or guaranteed employment. Either the school or the employee can terminate the employment relationship at any time, with or without cause, with or without notice. This is called **Employment at Will.**

This agreement becomes valid upon the official approval of the Principal, _____ and the _____ Board of Directors.
Sincerely,

_____   _____
Principal   Date

_____   _____
Employee Signature   Date

Examples of Daily Operational Plans

Daily Operational Plan
School
"Horseplay"
Date

Students will instructed, no later than two weeks after school has started, about the impropriety of "horseplay" on school property, to include any inappropriate touching, kicking, pushing, shoving or any other form of inappropriate physical contact which readily leads to more aggressive physical behavior on the part of either instigator or initial recipient of the action. Teachers should place added emphasis on this topic to avoid horseplay during transition periods, to include when students are moving from one class to another or when going up and down stairwells this school year. Furthermore, instruct your students that the penalties for "horseplay" will quickly accelerate from a verbal warning to much more serious consequences. The reduction of "horseplay" can dramatically reduce disciplinary problems in the upcoming school year, so your support of this policy is critical for its effective implementation.

Daily Operational Policy
School
Elevator Use
Date

Use of school elevators will be restricted to staff and/or official guests/visitors. Students will not be allowed to use the elevators under any circumstances other than when the school office is in possession of a doctor's note which indicates a medical necessity. Discipline for students who violate this policy will be swift and serious. The elevator will not normally be in use during the school day. A key to allow elevator operation is available in the school office when elevator for exigent circumstances. Mr. ....is the school's point of contact for elevator problems.

Daily Operational Policy
School
Morning Entry, Dismissal and Security Zone Monitoring
Date

Students may be dropped off at the front of the school from 7:30 A.M. onward. K-3 students will report to the school cafeteria, 4-6 students to the gym, for supervision by assigned staff members during this timeframe. Students will remain in their respectively assigned morning reception areas until 7:55 A.M., at which time they will be dismissed to go to class under the supervision of their first teacher of the morning.

Staff monitoring of identified school security zones will begin in the morning during the 7:30-7:55 A.M. time period and will recommence when school is dismissed.

At 3:15 P.M., after students are dismissed from classrooms, teachers will lock their classroom doors and either stand outside their rooms in the hallway to monitor student behavior or assume any assigned security zone monitoring position until 3:45 P.M. At 3:45 P.M. you may return to your room to conduct business as you see fit. Any student(s) remaining in your classroom area, not under your direct supervision, should be sent to the school office area for supervisory assistance.

Daily Operational Policy
School
Video Presentations
Date

In an effort to insure that proper instructional activities are being conducted on a continuing basis, effective this date, videos, with the exceptions noted at the bottom of this policy, will NOT be shown in any classroom setting unless they have been approved at least two days in advance by the Principal or a designated representative on the attached form.

In all cases, there MUST be an academic/educational connection between the video shown and the South Carolina standard course of study for that subject. Videos will NOT be shown solely for entertainment purposes or to take a break from teaching.

Videos will NOT be shown for "reward" or in place of a regular lesson plan. Animated videos will be given additional scrutiny. Cartoons such as "Sponge Bob Square Pants," should NEVER be shown to students due to their questionable educational value.

Video approval forms are available both in the office and in the teacher mailbox area. Videos should NEVER be shown in place of good teaching and should NOT be a frequent part of your classroom educational process.

Note: Video programming from PBS, ETV or another strictly education source do not require prior approval.

Video Approval Form
School

Title of Video You Request To Be Shown:

_____

Rating of Video: _____

APPROVED DISAPPROVED

_____

Signature Block
Principal
School

Daily Operational Policy
School
Detention
Date

In order for students to be fully successful in their classes, it is imperative that their homework be completed. Students who do not complete homework in a timely manner will be assigned detention by his or her teacher.

The teacher assigning detention will give the student and parents 48 hours so that prior arrangements can be made if necessary. During the detention, the student will make up missing homework assignments. Although the homework would then be completed, a ten point penalty will be assessed to those who completed the homework assignment on time.

Detention will not be served for work that cannot be made up nor will be served for large assignments such as a research paper.

Our intent is for students to not just be more responsible but, more importantly, to gain better of the "dynamics" in becoming a highly successful student.

Detention may still be assigned for misbehavior such as classroom disruptions. Although that is a separate issue, 24 hours will be given to students and parents before a detention is served.

Daily Operational Policy
School
Requirement for Service Learning
Date

Service learning is an education term used to describe youth learning in a school or community environment in which students perform socially needed tasks. Students are taught good citizenship and its application to academic subjects, skills and values. Service learning will be integrated into the school's core curriculum. Service learning engages young people in addressing significant unmet needs in their schools and communities. After these activities have taken place, students will subsequently analyze and reflect upon their experience.

Each grade level at .... will engage in at least one service learning project per school year. These activities will be documented on a form provided by the Principal. Classes can engage the rest of the school in their service learning activities if they so desire.

Some examples of service learning include, but are not limited to:

Reading to older adults at a nursing home
Raising funds to support schools in another country (e.g. "Pennies for Peace")
Collecting canned food for an animal shelter
Helping out at a community service organization like the Red Cross, Salvation Army, Goodwill, etc.
Collecting food for distribution to needy families.

These are just a few examples. Feel free to use your own imagination to figure out many, many more. The purpose of service learning is to engage our .... students in our community at large, to the point that they realize they are part of a much bigger whole.

Daily Operational Policy
School
Use/Possession of Cell Phones
Date

- Students may have cell phones at school, if they are kept in book bags or lockers and ARE NOT in an active/on status

- Cell phones MAY NOT BE USED BY STUDENTS AT ANY TIME DURING THE ACADEMIC SCHOOL DAY. If a student is found in possession of a cell phone during the academic school day, the cell phone will be confiscated and turned into the Principal or their designated representative.

- Students may turn on and use cell phones in the school building AFTER THEIR LAST ACADEMIC CLASS IS OVER AND THEY HAVE BEEN DISMISSED FROM THEIR FINAL CLASS OF THE DAY.

- A first offense of this policy will result in a one-time return of the cell phone to the student's parent/guardian at the end of the school day. A notation of this event will be kept in the Principal's office for future reference.

- Any second offense of illegal cell phone possession will result in confiscation of the student's cell phone for the remainder of the school year. This will be noted in the student's disciplinary file.

- Any student found in possession of a cell phone during any classroom testing environment will result in the cell phone being confiscated immediately. The use of a cell phone during testing comes is consider "cheating" and will receive consequences.

- Students will not use cell phones in the classroom in any other campus environment, to include bathroom facilities. If a student needs to the school to contact their parents, teachers will inform the office of this fact through the use of the intercom system (to be installed in December 2010). Again, use of a cell phone at any time during academic school hours is a violation of the school's disciplinary code.

Daily Operational Policy
School
Staff's Physical Presence on .... Campus
Date

Effectively immediately, ALL staff members will report to the school office at any time during the school day when it is their intent to leave campus. This includes during planning time or during lunch. Teachers will use the school's computer system for accountability purposes when either departing or returning to campus. Leaving campus and failing to use the school's computer system to sign in or out could result in serious disciplinary action.

At no time will teaching staff EVER leave campus with students in their classroom during scheduled instructional time, with any replacement filling in for you during your absence, without first receiving verbal approval from the Principal or their designated representative. Leaving campus with students in the classroom would only be considered for approval in light of a true family/medical emergency. Unless exigent circumstances exist and prior approval is issued by the Principal or their designated representative, any staff member violating this policy could expect termination of employment.

Daily Operational Policy
School
Distribution of Keys and/or Building Access Code
Date

Keys to any entrance to the school, to include the front door or any side door, will be signed out only after approval by the Principal. After approval by the Principal, Ms. ....will have the teacher sign the key sign-out sheet. If the key is returned, this will be noted on the key sign-out/in sheet.

Approval to obtain an access (alarm code) to the school will only be granted by the Principal. When an individual is given an access code, this will be noted on the key sign-out/in sheet along with any applicable key information.

There are no exceptions to this policy.

Daily Operational Policy
School
Business Environment in Front Office and/or on School Property During the
School Day
For All Employees (Instructional Staff and All Others)
Date

No discussions of school business, to include student discipline or staff personnel actions, should take place on the _____ campus unless it is between the Principal and staff members designated as being involved in decision making. These discussions will take place in a private setting. Parents, in particular, will be treated with the respect they are due, however, it is imperative that no student disciplinary or staff personnel issues be discussed with parents, visitors or former employees at any time to insure confidentiality.

Students are not allowed behind the front desk area unless a supervising adult is physically present to supervise them. This policy is effective immediately and staff members are expected to comply to insure that we present a professional appearance in the school office area.

Daily Operational Policy
School
Teaching/Licensure
Date

Effective this date, each and every classroom teacher will provide the Principal with a copy of their valid ....teaching license/certificate. If a teacher does not have a valid teaching license/certificate, they will provide a written memorandum to the Principal noting that fact. One copy of the documentation provided will be kept in the Principal's office in a licensure file, the other in the individual's official personnel file in the office.

Staff will provide this documentation to the Principal, in the noted applicable form, no later than _____. In addition, it is recommended that all staff members maintain a copy of their teaching license/certificate in their classroom for added security. When your license/certificate is renewed, you need to be sure to provide the Principal with a copy of that document.

There are no exceptions to this policy. In addition, personnel are reminded that it is their responsibility to insure that their teaching license/ certificate is kept current. For questions on licensure, please contact Ms. ....at................................... (contact person's name, telephone number and organization).

Daily Operational Policy
School
Non-Disparagement
Date

It is the policy of this school during the term of your employment and for one year thereafter, that you shall not in any communications with press, other media, any customer, client, supplier, student or parent of student, possible new student or their parent, criticize, ridicule, or make any statement that disparages or is derogatory of its administrators or its Board of Directors.

Acceptance of employment with .... implies that you will represent the school in a highly professional manner at all times, both on and off campus.

For further definition purposes, the word "disparaging" is defined as follows:

1, "to speak or treat slightingly; depreciate, belittle"

2. "to bring reproach or discredit upon; lower the estimation of"

Synonyms include:

Ridicule, discredit, mock, demean, denounce, derogate

Daily Operational Policy
School
Parties/Celebrations During the School Day
Date

Student birthday parties, etc. are fine, HOWEVER, they should take place in student homerooms, NOT in the cafeteria, since this causes a significant amount of distraction for students who are not participating, but want to, in the receipt of "goodies' in the form of cake or other such items.

Student parties WILL BE held in student homerooms to reduce disruption with daily instructional activities and/or in the amount of chaos that would be caused by being held in the cafeteria.

Be sure that there is enough of the food for everyone in the classroom or do not have the event and be sure that if there is diving up to do that everyone receives an equal portion. Who is in charge of distribution of the food item is simple; it must be someone (a parent of teacher) who will fairly distribute the food. If in doubt, do it yourself!

Daily Operational Policy
School
Student Seating Arrangements & General Classroom Interaction
Grades 4 up
Date

Student seating assignments come about in a variety of ways, e.g. teacher-directed, teacher-facilitated, via student-request, etc., but the purpose of this policy is simple, to ensure that students do not sit only with their chosen peer group to the exclusion of other students, but in an inclusive environment. Exclusion can come about in a variety of manners: to include through those who only want their friends near them; to be near those they feel are at their same academic functioning level, whether HIGH or LOW; or for other social, entirely appropriate personal reasons.

It is imperative that all students are treated equitably and that students do not take over the direction of the class through peer domination, which can be a qualifying factor for the initiation of bullying behavior. Please do not be naïve enough to believe that students will self-monitor themselves, they are going through a difficult period of adjustment in their lives and are often not capable of making entirely rational decisions, therefore we must, as adults, use our better-developed common sense to guide them.

In particular, if you are aware of concerns about group peer pressure in your classrooms and that students are being subjected to discriminating behavior because of their seat location in the classroom, you must effectively address this topic with great enthusiasm. I do not object to YOU making up a seating chart to disperse your students in a logical manner, keeping in mind you also have the option of changing seats on some sort of rotating basis. In many instances, what is currently in effect in SOME classes, letting students choose where they sit, is NOT WORKING and there is a resulting increase in negative student interaction.

This phenomenon of negativism seems to be in effect, at this time anyway, more for female than male students.

Finally, in regard to peer issues and general classroom interaction, YOU, the teacher should be the one who decides student grouping for classroom exercises and/or discussion groups. Our students have made it clear that when they have the choice, they will continually choose to participate with those in their immediate peer group, to the exclusion of others. This is NOT ACCEPTABLE. You are in charge, so do not turn over command of the classroom to those who are not mature enough to manage this issue. Our school philosophy does not endorse discrimination in any form and we need to ensure we do not support it in any way.

Daily Operational Policy
School
Work Hours/Reporting to Work/Departing
Date

Staff who have morning duties will report at the designated time, usually 7:30 A.M.

Instructional staff (classroom teachers) and other administrative personnel will report to the school no later than 7:45 A.M. each morning, whether or not you have a first period class or not.

Failure to be inside the school building at 7:45 A.M. will result in written counseling. Any subsequent tardies will result in more serious consequences, up to and including possible suspension or/and termination of employment with ....

In regard to departing the school at the end of the school day, if you are not tutoring until 4:45 P.M. you are employed to work until 3:45 P.M. unless you had morning duty, in which case you can depart as soon as possible after your children are dismissed.

If you have a "legitimate" excuse for being late, please present it immediately. It will be taken into consideration before any personnel action is taken.

Daily Operational Policy
School
Staff Supervision of Students During Classroom Transitions, at Lunch and at
Recess
Date

1. It is expected that all staff will be in the hallways, outside their classroom doors, during transitions in an effort to encourage and enforce proper student conduct.

2. During lunch, staff must disperse, seating-wise, throughout the cafeteria in order to provide proper supervision for all students.

3. At recess, staff members should take a particular "zone of participation" when providing outside supervision. Staff members should never congregate together in one place, but be in a position to keep all students within the view of one staff member or another at all times.

Daily Operational Policy
School
Planning/Approval of Field Trips
Date

Field Trips Within _____ County:

Two weeks notice required, in writing, to Principal. Do not start planning until the field trip has approved. Keep a copy of the signed approval.

Field Trips Outside of _____ County:

Four weeks' notice required, in writing, to Principal. Do not start planning until the field trip has been approved. Keep a copy of the signed approval.

For accountability purposes, no field trips should ever take place without the specific approval of the Principal, _____ Charter School.

Daily Operational Policy
School
Grade Drop Notification
Date

Teachers will contact parents/guardians by either by email, telephone calls or parent conference, when their child's academic grade significantly drops from a higher grade (e.g. "A" to a "C)" or from a "C" to an "D" or "F." This communication should be documented in the parent communication log you should keep in your classroom.

When you notice a decided downward trend in a student's academic achievement, you should contact their parent or guardian as soon as possible so that problem solving may be implemented.

Note: The reverse of "grade drop" is when a student is making significant improvement in their academic performance. There is no mandate on this, but it would contribute greatly to improved school/parent communication if you would call the parents with "good news" too!

Daily Operational Policy
School
Personnel Confidentiality
Date

All telephone communication from former employees will be routed to the Principal, _____ for action/resolution. Off campus, public discussions of school-related personnel actions in progress will be considered a breach of professional conduct. All emails from former employees about employment issues should immediately be referred to the Principal, _____ for proper action and should not be personally answered/responded to since a personal response represents a conflict of interest on the part of the staff member.

All matters brought to a staff member's attention that could have a potentially adverse effect on the school's reputation or the personal reputation of a current or former employee should be referred to the Principal, _____.

All information on on-going personnel issues will only be disseminated on a "need to know" basis.

Any violation of this policy will result in counseling or more negative personnel consequences.

Daily Operational Policy
School
Guidelines for Disciplinary Action
Date

Teachers are urged to encourage student self-discipline and too involved parents in student-related problem solving. In the event that differences cannot be resolved the classroom level, or violations of student behavior guidelines are observed, they will be referred to the Principal or his designated representative.

Violation of student behavior guidelines may result in short-term "time-outs," in-school suspension, short-term out of school suspension, a long-term out of school suspension or expulsion. The type and length of suspension will depend upon the severity of the violation, the circumstances of the situation and the professional judgment of the Principal, his designated representative or the Board of Directors. Other administrative actions may be contemplated in addition to suspension. ....will adhere to federal and state guidelines in all decisions regarding student suspension or expulsion.

The Principal will investigate any incident of violation of student behavior guidelines, hearing all versions of the fact. The student will be allowed to her the charges and evidence against him/her and present their version of the incident. The Principal will advise the student and his/her parents if a suspension is invoked, clearly informing them why the student is being suspended from school and for how long.

Any student suspended out of school is to remain off school grounds during the suspension period. Students are not allowed to attend any athletic events or extracurricular activities during the suspension period.

Suspension days apply only to days when school is in session for students. Teacher workdays, weekends, holidays and school days dismissed for weather do not count toward completion of a suspension assignment.

Short-Term In-School Suspension

The Principal may invoke a short-term in school suspension for a period of up to ten days for students who willingly violate the student behavior guidelines. Class assignments and tests will be provided to the student to complete during the in school suspension.

Short-Term Suspension

A "short-term suspension" is a suspension from school for 1-10 school days. This is a serious disciplinary action.

The Principal of _____ or his delegated representative shall have the authority to suspend for 10 days or less any student who willfully violates policies of conduct established by Spartanburg Charter School, contingent upon the fact that such a student suspended in this manner be provided the opportunity to take any quarterly, semester or grading period examinations missed during the suspension period.

Long-Term Suspension

A "long –term suspension" is a suspension from school for more than 10 school days. This is a serious disciplinary action and can extend through the end of the school year. Obviously, grades and course credit can be adversely affected.

The Principal of _____ has the authority to suspend for periods of time in excess of 10 school days but not exceeding the time remaining in the school year, any pupil who willfully violates the policies of conduct established by Spartanburg Charter School. The pupil and his/her parents may appeal the decision of the Principal to the Board of Directors.

The Principal will advise the students and his/her parents in writing by certified mail as to the nature of the incident(s) and the charges against the student which justify a long-term suspension. The parents will be informed in the written notice that within three days after notification they may request a hearing, wherein charges will be considered by a grievance committee appointed by the Board of Directors. In the notice the parents will be informed of the procedures and their rights. At the conclusion of the hearing, the board committee will recommend to the Board of Directors, on the basis of the evidence offered, if the punishment should be upheld or denied. The Board of Directors will notify the student and parents of their decision in writing.

Expulsion

An expulsion is the permanent exclusion of a student from school. The Board of Directors has the authority to expel a student from school with the recommendation from the Principal. Other alternative education methods will be considered before an expulsion is decided upon. The expelled student is permanently prohibited from returning to the school unless the Board of Directors reverses its decision. A student may apply for readmission, but not early than six months after their expulsion date. The same due process procedures apply as a long term suspension.

A student may be expelled only if: the continued presence of the student constitutes a clear threat to the safety and health of other students or school employees or disrupts learning to the point that other students are deprived of an education.

Any student suspended or expelled from school is to remain off school grounds for the duration of the expulsion period. Students may not attend any athletic events or extracurricular activities during this expulsion period.

Notwithstanding any law to the contrary, the Principal or Board of Directors of .... may refuse to admit any student who is suspended or expelled from any public school until the period of suspension or expulsion has expired.

Daily Operational Policy
School
Access to Students
Date

Anyone who comes to the school to either visit a student(s) or take a student(s) off of the campus (either temporarily or for the remainder of the day) must show identification and then be checked off as being listed on the student's "green card" filed in their cumulative folder in the school filing cabinets.

No "visitor" of any kind is to be allowed to proceed past the reception area and to have contact with any student, at any time, unless they have parental authorization noted on the aforementioned green card.

If any individual(s) present themselves at the office and verbally identify themselves as a relative (e.g. a grandfather or grandmother) and do not provide identification and are not subsequently noted on the green card, they will be denied entrance to the school facility until they are put on the approved list by that child's custodial parent(s). If they are not on the approved list, please politely deny them the right to enter the school facility at that time. If anyone makes an objection to not being allowed into the school facility to either visit or remove a child from campus, please contact the Principal or another Principal-designated staff member, immediately.

Daily Operational Policy
School
Student Retention Policy
Date

Documented exceptions to these procedures for ....may be made in special situations (e.g. special education students) with the approval of the school Principal.

1. If a student is failing to make normal progress, the parents must be notified early, so that the school and home may cooperate in helping him/her achieve greater success.

2. Most retentions should be at the primary level. However, older students may be considered if it is strongly felt retention will help the student.

3. No student shall be retained more than one year.

4. Light's Retention Scale must be completed prior to the teacher/Principal conference.

5. The teacher is to discuss possible retention with the school Principal prior to discussion with the parent.

6. A student retention worksheet and parent letter must be on file at the school for each student retained.

7. At the request of a parent, a review committee will be appointed to submit its recommendation to the Principal.

8. Parent notification of the recommendation to retain or accelerate is to be given as early as possible in the school year, but no later than the end of the first semester. Notification of possible retention is to include a note on the report card. Exceptions (e.g. late enrolling students, etc.) must have the school Principal's approval.

Daily Operational Policy
School
Cyber Bulling
Date

A Definition of Cyber Bullying

The use of any electronic device to threaten or harm another student constitutes Cyber Bullying as defined by _____. Cyber Bullying includes sending verbally threatening texts, photos or videos to another student, either while on campus or from any other location. Cyber Bullying includes, but is not limited to:

- Sending messages of a psychological or physically intimidating nature via any electronic medium, to anyone associated with _____.

- Posting information of a negative/inflammatory nature on a public website about any school-related individual, through any electronic medium

- Breaking into and/or misusing a school-assigned email account

- Providing/posting information, on-line, of a personal or inflammatory nature, about anyone associated with _____ on any electronic medium

Cyber Bullying will not be tolerated at _____ under any circumstances. Violations of this policy will be dealt with in timely manner, with the negative impact on the effected student kept in mind.

Daily Operational Policy
School
Student Attendance
Date

For attendance purposes, each three tardies equal one unexcused absence. It is imperative that students report to school on time (in the building no later than 8:00 A.M.) to ensure continuity of instruction.

Failure to meet compulsory .... attendance laws will result in the following sequence of consequences:

1. At ... Unexcused Absences: Letter of Concern sent home to parents

2. After .... Unexcused Absences: Letter of Warning (Retention possible due to excessive absences)

3. No Positive Response to Letter of Warning: Referral to Truancy Court

Daily Operational Policy
School
Disposition of Candy, Cakes or other Sugary Items in Classrooms
Date

Effective this date, teachers are no longer allowed to give out candy or other sweets to students in any form, to include as rewards or in "prize boxes" during the regular school day or when tutoring after school. With such a high obesity rate among children in this country today, we are not going to contribute to this phenomenon, hence cessation of the distribution of unhealthy food products.

Healthy, nutritional snacks such as granola bars may be given to students in place of items that contribute to obesity as long as this practice is done in moderation.

Daily Operational Policy
School
Personal Leave & Professional Development During Contract Time
Date

Instructional staff at this school will NOT be granted personal leave days (unless there are extraordinary circumstances, e.g. a death in the family) when professional development has been scheduled, in particular in the week (5-7 work days) prior to the start of school.

Staff should NOT attempt to schedule any personal engagements, to include weddings, vacations, etc. at times when professional development has been scheduled. A school calendar for the upcoming school year will be issued no later than March 1st of each school year and will note training days for that time period.

Failure to comply with this policy may result in consequences as serious as termination of employment. Your attendance at scheduled professional development is required under your contract.

APPENDIX L

Examples of Year One through Five Budgets

ABC Charter School
Updated Five-Year Budget

	FND	REVENUE	Revenues	FY-14	FY-15	FY-16	FY-17	FY-18
1	100	1920	Fundraising	$8,343	$8,510	$8,680	$8,854	$9,031
2	100	1999	Horry Electric Grant	$1,000	$1,020	$1,040	$1,061	$1,082
3	100	1910	Facility Rental	$60,000	$61,200	$62,424	$63,672	$64,946
4	100	3311	Education Finance Act (EFA)	$2,246,778	$2,333,333	$2,453,871	$2,572,075	$2,658,771
5	203	4510	IDEA (Regular)	$12,000	$14,000	$16,000	$18,000	$20,000
6	311	3511	Professional Development	$893	$901	$911	$920	$929
7	326	3526	Refurbish Science Kits	$1,200	$1,212	$1,224	$1,236	$1,249
8	338	3538	Students At Risk of School Failure	$30,585	$19,000	$19,000	$19,000	$19,000
9	344	3544	High Achieving Students	$8,793	$8,968	$9,148	$9,331	$9,517
10	350	3550	Teacher Salary Increase	$5,000	$5,100	$5,202	$5,306	$5,412
11	355	3555	School Employer Contributions	$1,000	$1,020	$1,040	$1,061	$1,082
12	358	3558	Reading	$712	$726	$741	$755	$771
13	377	3577	Teacher Supplies	$5,500	$5,500	$5,500	$5,500	$5,500
14	385	3585	Special Education (MOE)	$3,560	$0	$0	$0	$0
15	397	3597	Aid to Districts	$2,420	$2,468	$2,518	$2,568	$2,619
16	600	1610	Lunch Sales to Pupils	$21,000	$30,719	$31,747	$32,774	$33,288
17	600	4810	USDA Reimbursement - School Lunch	$20,000	$65,535	$67,727	$69,918	$71,014
18	700	1700	Pupil Activity	$32,500	$46,943	$48,513	$50,083	$50,868
19	928	3118	EEDA Career Specialists	$2,416	$2,464	$2,513	$2,563	$2,615
20	933	3123	Formative Assesment	$700	$714	$728	$743	$758
21	937	3127	Student Health & Fitness	$1,774	$1,809	$1,845	$1,882	$1,920
22	960	3610	K-5 Enhancement	$6,976	$7,046	$7,117	$7,188	$7,260
23	967	3607	6-8 Enhancement	$470	$475	$479	$484	$489
24			**Total Revenue**	$2,473,618	$2,618,664	$2,747,967	$2,874,976	$2,968,121

1

ABC Charter School
Updated Five-Year Budget

	FND	FCT	OBJ	Instruction Expenditures	FY-14	FY-15	FY-16	FY-17	FY-18
25	100	110	110	Teacher Salaries	$782,693	$813,507	$837,912	$863,049	$888,941
26	100	110	120	Substitute Pay	$9,000	$9,000	$9,000	$9,000	$9,000
27	100	110	210	Group Health & Life Insurance	$84,344	$98,487	$101,441	$105,499	$109,719
28	100	110	220	Employee Retirement	$121,474	$126,256	$130,044	$133,945	$137,964
29	100	110	230	Social Security	$60,564	$62,922	$64,789	$66,712	$68,692
30	100	110	260	Unemployment Compensation Tax	$13,056	$7,480	$7,480	$7,480	$7,480
31	100	110	270	Worker's Compensation Tax	$7,749	$8,054	$8,295	$8,544	$8,801
32	100	110	311	Instructional Services	$33,500	$36,500	$38,000	$39,500	$41,000
33	100	110	410	Instructional Supplies	$30,000	$74,750	$77,250	$79,750	$81,000
34	377	110	410	Teacher Supplies	$5,500	$5,500	$5,500	$5,500	$5,500
35	100	110	420	Instructional Textbooks	$5,000	$6,000	$7,000	$8,000	$9,000
36	100	110	540	Instructional Equipment	$45,000	$15,000	$15,000	$15,000	$15,000
37	100	110	545	Instructional Computers	$20,000	$15,000	$15,000	$15,000	$15,000
38	100	188	313	Parenting	$7,200	$7,500	$7,800	$8,100	$8,400
39				**Total Instruction Expense**	**$1,225,079**	**$1,285,955**	**$1,324,511**	**$1,365,079**	**$1,405,496**

	FND	FCT	OBJ	Support Services Expenditures	FY-14	FY-15	FY-16	FY-17	FY-18
40	100	214	313	Psychological Services	$4,300	$4,600	$4,900	$5,200	$5,500
41	100	215	313	SP Services	$18,000	$34,000	$36,000	$38,000	$40,000
42	203	215	313	SP Services	$12,000	$12,000	$12,000	$12,000	$12,000
43	100	215	313	EC Program Consulting	$12,000	$13,000	$14,000	$15,000	$16,000
44	100	221	110	Curriculum Development Salaries	$55,000	$65,000	$66,000	$67,980	$70,019
45	100	221	220	Employee Retirement	$8,536	$10,088	$10,243	$10,550	$10,867
46	100	221	230	Social Security	$4,208	$4,973	$5,049	$5,200	$5,356
47	100	221	260	Unemployment Compensation Tax	$408	$340	$340	$340	$340
48	100	221	270	Worker's Compensation Tax	$545	$644	$653	$673	$693
49	100	224	312	Professional Development	$14,500	$15,000	$15,500	$16,000	$16,500

2

ABC Charter School
Updated Five-Year Budget

	FND	FCT	OBJ	Support Services Expenditures	FY-14	FY-15	FY-16	FY-17	FY-18
50	100	231	318	Audit Services	$15,300	$15,700	$16,100	$16,500	$16,500
51	100	231	319	Legal Services	$1,000	$2,000	$2,500	$3,000	$3,500
52	100	231	640	Membership Dues & Fees	$3,000	$3,000	$3,000	$3,000	$3,000
53	100	231	650	Liability Insurance	$8,685	$9,032	$9,394	$9,769	$10,160
54	100	233	111	Principal Salaries	$104,500	$89,057	$91,729	$94,481	$97,315
55	100	233	115	Administrative Assistant Salaries	$26,786	$28,837	$29,702	$30,593	$31,511
56	100	233	210	Group Health & Life Insurance	$14,939	$15,848	$16,324	$16,977	$17,656
57	100	233	220	Employee Retirement	$20,376	$18,297	$18,846	$19,411	$19,994
58	100	233	230	Social Security	$10,043	$9,019	$9,289	$9,568	$9,855
59	100	233	260	Unemployment Compensation Tax	$680	$680	$680	$680	$680
60	100	233	270	Worker's Compensation Tax	$1,300	$1,167	$1,202	$1,238	$1,275
61	100	233	332	Travel	$7,200	$7,500	$7,700	$7,900	$8,100
62	100	233	410	Office Supplies	$10,000	$11,000	$12,000	$13,000	$14,000
63	100	233	540	Office Equipment	$11,500	$12,000	$12,500	$13,000	$13,500
64	100	252	315	Fiscal Services	$39,960	$40,365	$41,715	$43,065	$43,740
65	100	252	690	Bank Fees	$700	$720	$740	$780	$800
66	100	254	110	Custodial Salary	$17,041	$21,628	$22,277	$22,945	$23,633
67	100	254	210	Group Health & Life	$1,975	$6,115	$6,298	$6,550	$6,812
68	100	254	220	Employee Retirement	$2,645	$3,357	$3,457	$3,561	$3,668
69	100	254	230	Social Security	$1,304	$1,655	$1,704	$1,755	$1,808
70	100	254	260	Unemployment Compensation Tax	$408	$340	$340	$340	$340
71	100	254	270	Worker's Compensation Tax	$169	$214	$221	$227	$234
72	100	254	321	Public Utility Services (Water & Sewer)	$4,000	$4,120	$4,244	$4,371	$4,502
73	100	254	323	Repairs & Maintenance Services	$5,000	$6,000	$7,000	$8,000	$9,000
74	100	254	324	Property Insurance	$5,200	$5,408	$5,624	$5,849	$6,083
75	100	254	325	Facility Lease	$513,256	$515,000	$515,000	$515,000	$515,000
76	100	254	329	Trash	$2,000	$2,060	$2,122	$2,185	$2,251
77	100	254	340	Telephone	$10,500	$11,000	$11,500	$12,000	$12,500
78	100	254	410	Building Supplies	$20,000	$21,000	$22,000	$23,000	$24,000
79	100	254	470	Energy (Electric, Gas, Oil)	$35,000	$36,750	$38,588	$40,517	$42,543

3

ABC Charter School
Updated Five-Year Budget

	FND	FCT	OBJ	Support Services Expenditures	FY-14	FY-15	FY-16	FY-17	FY-18
80	100	255	110	Bus Driver Salaries	$3,600	$3,708	$3,819	$3,934	$4,052
81	100	255	230	Social Security	$275	$284	$292	$301	$310
82	100	255	260	Unemployment Compensation Tax	$122	$130	$130	$130	$130
83	100	255	270	Worker's Compensation Tax	$36	$37	$38	$39	$40
84	100	255	331	Student Transportation Services	$1,000	$1,300	$1,600	$1,800	$2,000
85	100	255	650	Vehicle Liability	$216	$225	$234	$243	$253
86	100	258	329	Building Security Maintenance	$11,000	$12,000	$13,000	$14,000	$15,000
87	100	263	350	Marketing & Advertising	$500	$5,000	$6,000	$7,000	$8,000
88	100	266	345	Technology Services	$1,300	$5,500	$6,000	$6,500	$7,000
89	100	271	660	Field Trips	$8,500	$9,000	$9,500	$10,000	$10,500
90	600	256	110	Food Service Salaries	$43,040	$44,331	$45,661	$47,031	$48,442
91	600	256	210	Group Health & Life Insurance	$9,315	$9,688	$10,075	$10,478	$10,897
92	600	256	220	Employee Retirement	$6,680	$6,880	$7,087	$7,299	$7,518
93	600	256	230	Social Security	$3,293	$3,391	$3,493	$3,598	$3,706
94	600	256	260	Unemployment Compensation Tax	$2,448	$2,040	$1,360	$1,360	$1,360
95	600	256	270	Worker's Compensation Tax	$426	$439	$452	$466	$480
96	600	256	460	Food Purchases	$50,000	$85,000	$90,000	$95,000	$100,000
97	600	256	540	Food Equipment	$16,000	$9,000	$5,000	$5,000	$5,000
98				**Total Support Services Expense**	**$1,181,712**	**$1,256,466**	**$1,282,223**	**$1,314,387**	**$1,345,925**
99				**Total Expenditures**	**$2,406,791**	**$2,542,421**	**$2,606,734**	**$2,679,467**	**$2,751,421**
100				**Budget Balance**	**$66,827**	**$76,243**	**$141,233**	**$195,509**	**$216,699**

4

APPENDIX M

Sample Monthly Budget for Charter Schools

ABC Charter School
Monthly Budget Report

	FND	REVENUE	Revenues	Budget	Month-to-Date	Year-to-Date	Remaining	%
1	100	1920	Fundraising	$8,343.20	$5,725.11	$8,343.20	$0.00	0.00%
2	100	1999	Horry Electric Grant	$1,000.00	$1,000.00	$1,000.00	$0.00	0.00%
3	100	1999	Facility Rent	$60,000.00	$10,000.00	$30,000.00	$30,000.00	50.00%
4	100	3311	Education Finance Act (EFA)	$2,246,777.85	$187,231.49	$936,157.44	$1,310,620.41	58.33%
5	203	4510	IDEA (Regular)	$12,000.00	$4,000.00	$6,000.00	$6,000.00	50.00%
6	311	3511	Professional Development	$892.56	$0.00	$297.52	$595.04	66.67%
7	318	3518	Formative Assessment	$700.00	$0.00	$0.00	$700.00	100.00%
8	326	3526	Refurbish Science Kits	$1,200.00	$1,200.00	$1,200.00	$0.00	0.00%
9	338	3538	Students At Risk of School Failure	$30,585.03	$0.00	$20,195.01	$10,390.02	33.97%
10	344	3544	High Achieving Students	$8,792.55	$0.00	$2,930.85	$5,861.70	66.67%
11	350	3550	Teacher Salary Increase	$5,000.00	$2,500.00	$2,500.00	$2,500.00	50.00%
12	355	3555	School Employer Contributions	$1,000.00	$500.00	$500.00	$500.00	50.00%
13	358	3558	Reading	$711.84	$0.00	$237.28	$474.56	66.67%
14	377	3577	Teacher Supplies	$5,500.00	$825.00	$5,500.00	$0.00	0.00%
15	385	3585	Special Education (MOE)	$3,559.98	$0.00	$1,186.66	$2,373.32	66.67%
16	397	3597	Aid to Districts	$2,419.80	$0.00	$806.60	$1,613.20	66.67%
17	600	1610	Lunch Sales to Pupils	$21,000.00	$3,805.00	$10,954.40	$10,045.60	47.84%
18	600	4810	USDA Reimbursement - School Lunch	$20,000.00	$2,437.77	$7,304.31	$12,695.69	63.48%
19	700	1700	Pupil Activity	$32,500.00	$3,523.05	$26,187.66	$6,312.34	19.42%
20	928	3118	EEDA Career Specialists	$2,415.51	$0.00	$805.17	$1,610.34	66.67%
21	937	3127	Student Health & Fitness	$1,773.63	$0.00	$591.21	$1,182.42	66.67%
22	960	3610	K-5 Enhancement	$6,976.44	$0.00	$2,325.48	$4,650.96	66.67%
23	967	3607	6-8 Enhancement	$470.00	$0.00	$235.00	$235.00	50.00%
24			Total Revenue	$2,473,618.39	$222,747.42	$1,065,257.79	$1,408,360.60	56.94%

1

ABC Charter School
Monthly Budget Report

	FND	FCT	OBJ	Instruction Expenditures	Budget	Month-to-Date	Year-to-Date	Remaining	%
25	100	110	110	Teacher Salaries	$782,692.50	$68,914.52	$300,290.81	$482,401.69	61.63%
26	100	110	120	Substitute Pay	$9,000.00	$1,162.50	$3,000.00	$6,000.00	66.67%
27	100	110	210	Group Health & Life Insurance	$84,343.51	$12,885.73	$34,856.00	$49,487.51	58.67%
28	100	110	220	Employee Retirement	$121,473.88	$10,184.96	$43,613.63	$77,860.25	64.10%
29	100	110	230	Social Security	$60,564.48	$5,104.76	$23,725.46	$36,839.02	60.83%
30	100	110	260	Unemployment Compensation Tax	$13,056.00	$0.00	$6,245.82	$6,810.18	52.16%
31	100	110	270	Worker's Compensation Tax	$7,748.66	$0.00	$2,887.43	$4,861.23	62.74%
32	100	110	311	Instructional Services	$33,500.00	$75.00	$512.00	$32,988.00	98.47%
33	100	110	410	Instructional Supplies	$30,000.00	$471.75	$29,342.57	$657.43	2.19%
34	377	110	410	Teacher Supplies	$5,500.00	$0.00	$5,225.00	$275.00	5.00%
35	100	110	420	Instructional Textbooks	$5,000.00	$0.00	$0.00	$5,000.00	100.00%
36	252	110	540	Instructional Equipment	$45,000.00	$1,000.00	$5,521.92	$39,478.08	87.73%
37	100	110	545	Instructional Cap Computers	$20,000.00	$0.00	$10,028.10	$9,971.90	49.86%
38	100	188	313	Parenting	$7,200.00	$0.00	$0.00	$7,200.00	100.00%
39				Total Instruction Expense	$1,225,079.02	$99,799.22	$465,248.74	$759,830.28	62.02%

2

ABC Charter School
Monthly Budget Report

	FND	FCT	OBJ	Support Services Expenditures	Budget	Month-to-Date	Year-to-Date	Remaining	%
40	100	214	313	Psychological Services	$4,300.00	$0.00	$0.00	$4,300.00	100.00%
41	100	215	313	LD Services	$0.00	$0.00	$0.00	$0.00	0.00%
42	203	215	313	LD Services	$0.00	$0.00	$0.00	$0.00	0.00%
43	100	215	313	SP Services	$18,000.00	$0.00	$0.00	$18,000.00	100.00%
44	203	215	313	SP Services	$12,000.00	$0.00	$5,986.00	$6,014.00	50.12%
45	100	215	313	EC Program Consulting	$12,000.00	$0.00	$0.00	$12,000.00	100.00%
46	100	221	110	Curriculum Development Salaries	$55,000.00	$4,583.34	$22,916.70	$32,083.30	58.33%
47	100	221	210	Group Health & Life Insurance	$0.00	$0.00	$0.00	$0.00	0.00%
48	100	221	220	Employee Retirement	$8,536.00	$711.32	$3,556.60	$4,979.40	58.33%
49	100	221	230	Social Security	$4,207.50	$337.32	$1,727.10	$2,480.40	58.95%
50	100	221	260	Unemployment Compensation Tax	$408.00	$0.00	$0.00	$408.00	100.00%
51	100	221	270	Worker's Compensation Tax	$544.50	$0.00	$0.00	$544.50	100.00%
52	100	224	312	Professional Development	$14,500.00	$298.00	$5,602.27	$8,897.73	61.36%
53	100	231	318	Audit Services	$15,300.00	$0.00	$12,290.00	$3,010.00	19.67%
54	100	231	319	Legal Services	$1,000.00	$0.00	$0.00	$1,000.00	100.00%
55	100	231	410	Fundraising Supplies	$0.00	$0.00	$0.00	$0.00	0.00%
56	100	231	640	Membership Dues & Fees	$3,000.00	$0.00	$840.00	$2,160.00	72.00%
57	100	231	650	Liability Insurance	$8,684.96	$0.00	$8,684.50	$0.46	0.01%
58	100	233	111	Principal Salaries	$104,500.00	$7,041.66	$55,208.30	$49,291.70	47.17%
59	100	233	111	Assistant Principal Salaries	$0.00	$0.00	$0.00	$0.00	0.00%
60	100	233	115	Administrative Assistant Salaries	$26,786.00	$2,620.00	$11,043.30	$15,742.70	58.77%
61	100	233	210	Group Health & Life Insurance	$14,938.54	$1,284.40	$6,382.12	$8,556.42	57.28%
62	100	233	220	Employee Retirement	$20,375.59	$1,499.48	$7,178.21	$13,197.38	64.77%
63	100	233	230	Social Security	$10,043.38	$661.89	$3,169.94	$6,873.44	68.44%
64	100	233	260	Unemployment Compensation Tax	$680.00	$0.00	$0.00	$680.00	100.00%
65	100	233	270	Worker's Compensation Tax	$1,299.73	$0.00	$0.00	$1,299.73	100.00%
66	100	233	311	Contracted Admin Services	$0.00	$0.00	$0.00	$0.00	0.00%
67	100	233	332	Travel	$7,200.00	$0.00	$673.12	$6,526.88	90.65%
68	100	233	410	Office Supplies	$10,000.00	$42.00	$5,741.93	$4,258.07	42.58%
69	100	233	540	Office Equipment	$11,500.00	$0.00	$2,785.38	$8,714.62	75.78%

3

ABC Charter School
Monthly Budget Report

	FND	FCT	OBJ	Support Services Expenditures	Budget	Month-to-Date	Year-to-Date	Remaining	%
70	100	252	315	Fiscal Services	$39,960.00	$1,732.50	$8,662.50	$31,297.50	78.32%
71	100	252	690	Bank Fees	$700.00	$93.00	$370.05	$329.95	47.14%
72	100	253	395	Architectural Services	$0.00	$0.00	$0.00	$0.00	0.00%
73	100	253	520	Construction Services	$0.00	$0.00	$0.00	$0.00	0.00%
74	100	254	110	Custodial Salary	$17,041.10	$817.38	$6,821.10	$10,220.00	59.97%
75	100	254	210	Group Health & Life Insurance	$1,974.64	$0.00	$1,974.64	$0.00	0.00%
76	100	254	220	Employee Retirement	$2,644.78	$73.08	$1,004.85	$1,639.93	62.01%
77	100	254	230	Social Security	$1,303.64	$59.84	$370.03	$933.61	71.62%
78	100	254	260	Unemployment Compensation Tax	$408.00	$0.00	$0.00	$408.00	100.00%
79	100	254	270	Worker's Compensation Tax	$168.71	$0.00	$0.00	$168.71	100.00%
80	100	254	321	Public Utility Services (Water & Sewer)	$4,000.00	$131.25	$939.70	$3,060.30	100.00%
81	100	254	323	Repairs & Maintenance Services	$5,000.00	$150.00	$1,371.57	$3,628.43	72.57%
82	100	254	324	Property Insurance	$5,200.00	$0.00	$2,493.36	$2,706.64	52.05%
83	100	254	325	Facility Lease	$513,255.65	$95,000.00	$233,379.15	$279,876.50	54.53%
84	100	254	329	Trash Service	$2,000.00	$0.00	$523.28	$1,476.72	73.84%
85	100	254	340	Telephone	$10,500.00	$642.69	$4,495.10	$6,004.90	57.19%
86	100	254	410	Building Supplies	$20,000.00	$0.00	$9,989.29	$10,010.71	50.05%
87	100	254	470	Energy (Electric, Gas, Oil)	$35,000.00	$10,175.28	$16,265.11	$18,734.89	100.00%
88	100	255	110	Bus Driver Salaries	$3,600.00	$150.00	$300.00	$3,300.00	91.67%
89	100	255	230	Social Security	$275.40	$11.47	$22.95	$252.45	91.67%
90	100	255	260	Unemployment Compensation Tax	$122.40	$0.00	$0.00	$122.40	100.00%
91	100	255	270	Worker's Compensation Tax	$35.64	$0.00	$0.00	$35.64	100.00%
92	100	255	331	Student Transportation Services	$1,000.00	$82.15	$291.43	$708.57	70.86%
93	100	255	650	Vehicle Liability	$216.30	$0.00	$0.00	$216.30	100.00%
94	100	258	329	Building Security Maintenance	$11,000.00	$0.00	$10,154.20	$845.80	7.69%
95	100	263	350	Marketing & Advertising	$500.00	$0.00	$0.00	$500.00	100.00%
96	100	266	345	Technology Services	$1,300.00	$0.00	$655.00	$645.00	49.62%
97	100	271	660	Field Trips	$8,500.00	$1,259.71	$2,496.84	$6,003.16	70.63%

4

ABC Charter School
Monthly Budget Report

	FND	FCT	OBJ	Support Services Expenditures	Budget	Month-to-Date	Year-to-Date	Remaining	%
98	600	256	110	Food Service Salaries	$43,040.00	$3,918.00	$13,375.20	$29,664.80	68.92%
99	600	256	210	Group Health & Life Insurance	$9,315.22	$793.56	$1,622.28	$7,692.94	82.58%
100	600	256	220	Employee Retirement	$6,679.81	$497.91	$1,759.22	$4,920.59	73.66%
101	600	256	230	Social Security	$3,292.56	$251.44	$874.90	$2,417.66	73.43%
102	600	256	260	Unemployment Compensation Tax	$2,448.00	$0.00	$0.00	$2,448.00	100.00%
103	600	256	270	Worker's Compensation Tax	$426.10	$0.00	$0.00	$426.10	100.00%
104	600	256	391	Contracted Food Services	$0.00	$0.00	$0.00	$0.00	0.00%
105	600	256	460	Food Purchases	$50,000.00	$24.56	$20,886.17	$29,113.83	58.23%
106	600	256	540	Food Equipment	$16,000.00	$0.00	$15,532.16	$467.84	2.92%
107				**Total Support Services Expense**	**$1,181,712.14**	**$134,943.23**	**$510,415.55**	**$671,296.59**	**56.81%**
108				**Total Expenditures**	**$2,406,791.17**	**$234,742.45**	**$975,664.29**	**$1,431,126.88**	**59.46%**
109				**FY-14 Budget Balance**	**$66,827.22**	**($11,995.03)**	**$89,593.50**		
110				FY-13 Cash Balance	$649,741.42		$649,741.42		
111				FY-13 Accounts Receivable	$7,130.75		$7,130.75		
112				FY-13 Accounts Payable	($15,615.03)		($15,615.03)		
113				Legal Settlement	($20,000.00)		($20,000.00)		
114				**FY-14 Fund Balance**	**$688,084.36**		**$710,850.64**		

5

APPENDIX N

Examples of Investigations in a School Setting

Case #1

Alleged Thefts on School Property

"The Missing CD's"

One of the first things to remember is that teachers, just like students, are imperfect beings and subject to human error when reporting objects or personal property to be missing from their classrooms. Once you investigate quite a few cases of missing objects from the classroom, you will often come to the realization that property is just as likely to have been misplaced as stolen. Unless you can find a witness to a theft of a teacher's property from the classroom or another defined area, the best you can do is to assume a theft took place, until some other outcome is established. Why have any doubts at all when a teacher reports something stolen? Have you ever misplaced your wallet, purse or keys and been sure you left them on the coffee table, only to find them somewhere else?

Before you spend an inordinate amount of time interviewing possible suspects, be sure you conduct a thorough interview of the teacher first, getting all of the possible details of their possible movements that day, to include the last place the object was seen, where it was in the room, who was in the general area at the time, what the timeframe was for the alleged theft, etc. In other words, ask who, what, when, where and why so you are able to conduct a competent investigation. Don't forget to ask if anyone else (a trusted person) can also verify the item's presence at a set time and place to add credibility to a claim of theft. It is unfortunate that teachers often do not report items missing until the next period, after students have left the room, which greatly reduces the possibility of conducting a meaningful search. I have never conducted a random search of student lockers, even though I would very likely have had the authority to do so, since I consider this too intrusive (surprise!)

What follows are the facts presented in one real life case. A teacher reported that during second period (9:30 – 11:00 A.M.), on the previous day, her six DVD collection on "Animal Life on Planet Earth" was stolen from the top of her desk. The first thing you need to disregard is any thought of scolding this teacher for leaving out the DVD's in the first place; this will not achieve anything positive, but may cause some actual animosity.

In this teacher's case, several reliable students verified the presence of the DVD's her desktop, so we truly believed a theft of personal property had taken place. Now, what to do next, a day after the DVD's had disappeared? The first thing I did was to sit down and develop an investigative plan. I interviewed the reporting teacher during her first available break that day in regard to whether she had left the door to her classroom open at any time when she was out of the room and students were present. She answered "yes," that two female students were left in the room while she went to the bathroom. This is not evidence they stole the DVD's, however it does identify the fact they had a unique opportunity others did not have. What transpired next became a tangled web indeed.

Once again remembering that mere suspicion, even in conjunction with opportunity do not equal evidence, interviews of the girls were conducted, each of them very low key in nature, with absolutely no accusations being made. Each girl was interviewed separately and each emphatically denied any knowledge of the matter, to include ever seeing the DVD collection in the room or any desire to own DVD's about this specific subject matter (animals). I was unconvinced.

Later that day, after the girls had obviously had an opportunity to go home, one parent called me to complain that I had interviewed his daughter about the alleged theft. I advised them that one of my responsibilities as Principal was to investigate the disappearance of a teacher's property. I then mentioned the topic of the DVD collection at which time the parent exclaimed "my daughter likes animal videos" and furthermore that she had a DVD collection of that nature at home. I then asked how long she ago she had purchased it or if someone had bought it for her, The tone of the parent's voice quickly changed and he got very upset, stating he was not going to answer any more of my questions. In an effort to ensure this was not a coincidence, I made one last ditch effort and asked the parent if their daughter could bring the DVD's to school so we prove we this was just a coincidence? The parent then hung up the phone on me. This is the closest to solving the case of the missing DVD's we ever got; however there were no more thefts from this teacher's classroom at in the next three years.

What is the easiest way to prove who stolen something in a school setting? Develop a good relationship with all of your students, one in which they will willingly provide you with information, to include "who did it." If you encourage a spirit of mutual respect among your students population, your students will not want to have thieves amongst them in their school community, knowing that with them there they themselves might be the next victim.

Case#2

Alleged Vandalism of Property

"Seeking Revenge?"

One Sunday morning, I received a telephone call from an Assistant Principal, somewhat hysterically reporting to me that someone had broken into a classroom and urinated on a teacher's personal chair. The first thing I said was "relax; I'll be there in a few minutes." One of the most important things I learned from my mentors (to include Special Agents who had worked on national-level, high-profile investigations), was to not overreact when you first receive notification about an incident. As an example of this, I distinctly recall a call coming into the USACIDC Field Office at Fort Jackson to report a body being found about two blocks away. The next thing that happened was that three carloads of Special Agents jumped into their cars to go to the crime scene, only to get there and realize they and left their crime scene processing kits back at the office (no, not all federal agents have "CSI-type" people to back them up, they have to do their own collection of evidence at crime scenes). My Operations Officer laughed when the agents returned to the office. He then gave them some very sound advice: "Next time, sit down, have a cup coffee and develop a plan of action before leaving for the scene." The point I am doing my best to make is that it is important to be patient and plan before you take action, no matter what the implications might be: personal, political or otherwise.

Now, let's return to the classroom. Have you ever heard the theory that offenders frequently return to the scene of the crime? From my experience, both as a federal agent and school administrator, I believe this to be a truism, which is why, post-offense; videos are often taken of crowds at crime scenes.

When I first got to the campus that morning, I went to the back of the school, only to find other school administrators and the teacher whose room had been "violated" present. Knowing me from past experiences, no one had entered the room; so I knew they had listened to me when I had talked to them in the past about the proper way to secure any crime scene. There were no signs of forced entry into the room and the teacher adamantly stated that the windows were always secured when she left on Fridays. Knowing students can be tricky in their own right, I concluded that window did not open itself, that there had to be an "insider" who left the window open, that this was not the job of a "professional" and that they could have left fingerprints on the window. So, what would I do next, believing this theory to be true? I went to the nearest copy machine, opened it up and poured some toner cartridge powder into a small box. Next, I went to the art room and borrowed a small paint brush and a roll of scotch tape. I then returned to the outside of the classroom (which was still secured on the inside), put some of the cartridge powder on the paint brush and "dusted the window," only to find there were no discernible fingerprints on the window. Well, I never said I am always right, so I proceeded to put my own fingerprint on the window, dust my prints, put scotch tape over the print, lift it from the window, put the lifted print on a 3x5 card and, finally, into an envelope. I'm sure my staff standing nearby wondered exactly what I was doing, so I advised them, step by step, in a very loud voice, how I was securing evidence from the crime scene. We then proceeded into the room in to search for other evidence about who entered the room illegally, wrote on the whiteboard and urinated on the teacher's chair. Unfortunately, we found none. So….

The next morning at school, I again asked the teacher whose room had been vandalized if she had made enemies among students in her class, to which she replied "absolutely not." My gut instinct again told me she was either naïve or just hesitant to admit she had irritated one of her students to the point they would commit an offense of this nature against her. When someone takes the time to urinate on your personal chair it is obvious it isn't a random act; but one with a distinct component of personal malice. If you watch enough television, you will always hear that when someone is stabbed multiple times "it was personal" because random acts do not show the same intensity of effort.

It will not, however, do you any good to mimic detectives on television when they say they routinely solve crimes by "thinking like the offenders." Unless you are a forensic psychologist or a criminal investigator, this is a very difficult task to master. Since this incident of vandalism was so bold and brazen, I put the word out to several very talkative students I knew who could not keep their mouths shut. This is an example of the successful use of useful propaganda in a school setting. Word quickly spread that fingerprints had been successfully lifted from the outside window and "elsewhere' (I had not given this information to the students) and lo and behold, within thirty minutes a female high school student came to my office with a request to speak to me. Before I could even ask her to sit down she blurted out "I was there, with them, but I didn't go into the room," followed by "I don't want to go to jail, I know you have our fingerprints!" I advised her that if she provided me with reliable information this "could be" taken into consideration. Note: I do not, nor ever have I, promised a suspect anything, to include leniency. This is never a good practice for either federal agent or school administrator. She proceeded to identify a male student in the concerned teacher's class as the one who had opened a classroom window at the end of the school day on Friday; followed by the admission that two of her friends from a local private school were the ones who had written the profanity on the whiteboard and urinated on the chair, these acts perpetrated on behalf of their male friend who felt he had been mistreated by the teacher. I took a written statement documenting her testimony, which she eagerly signed. This became key evidence in my investigation.

After identifying the male perpetrator who opened the window as a result of this young lady's testimony, I located the boy and had him escorted to my office by one of my Assistant Principals. Once he was in my office and sat down, I did not ask him if he had opened the window, I told him I knew he did, which dispensed with all back and forth banter that would have surely included accusations on my part and denials from him. The most important point to remember here is that I knew he opened the window. With this knowledge in hand, there was absolutely no hesitation on my part to openly identify the part he played in the commission of the offense. If you express a lack of assurance, a student will recognize this and could be hesitant to admit their culpability. By the way, the lifted fingerprints (mine) were lying on the table in front of me when while we spoke. I never had to comment on them during the course of our verbal interaction.

The first words out of his mouth, after my statement regarding his willing participation in this offense were "I only opened the window!" which verified what I had already been told. My next question was "Who else was involved in this?" To my amazement, he instantly named the two students from the local private school as being the ones who went into the room. When I asked him to provide me with a rationale or motive for this event, he stated he felt the teacher had been "mean" to him, she deserved it and further that his friends felt bad for him and offered to help him exact his revenge on her, hence the very personal act of urinating on her personal chair in the classroom.

Okay, they were friends, but there had to be something more. Their apparent connection, public and private school students, was not enough to satisfy my curiosity. Realizing he had already committed to telling the truth about his part in this offense, he related that he and the others attended the same church, some one hundred yards across a field from the high school where the offenses had taken place. Then he dropped the "bombshell" on me, stating that all of them had returned to the church on Sunday and were physically present, observing, while my staff and I were "processing the crime scene." There is not a lot of difference between student criminals and their adult versions; they like to see the fruits of their labor in the form of who gets riled up by their illegal pursuits. While some school administrators might have called the police in regard to this matter, I took the simple, more expeditious approach, knowing that this offense would be rated a very low priority by them and that I knew my students better than they did. The end result of this investigation was that I spoke to the Headmaster at the private school the two boys attended and they were expelled (they readily confessed to the Headmaster rather than be subjected to criminal prosecution). The male who opened the window moved to another city with his parents and the girl who provided all of the details continued to attend our school without anyone ever knowing she acted as an informant. Her identity was kept confidential in the event she was needed as a resource in the future. And, who says the punishment must always fit the crime? Why handle this matter the way I did versus calling the police? I believe that because kids do "dumb stuff" and frequently use bad judgment, they do not necessarily need a police record. The fact that nothing was stolen from the room also influenced my decision making. The students did pay for the cost of having the teacher's personal chair replaced.

Case#3
Alleged Sexual Abuse of Students by Staff
"The Lesser of Two Evils"

In 2004, as a Principal, I had my first opportunity to apply the "Lesser of Two Evils" technique. While in my office one day, one of my Assistant Principals came to me, extremely flustered, muttering below his breath "You're not going to believe this!" What followed was a story about how a male high school teacher had allegedly lured a ninth grade female student to his empty classroom under false pretenses, hugged her, kissed her and put his hands in her pants. The teacher who allegedly committed this offence was one we all considered an "All-Star" teacher, a role model for young men. I completely understood why the Assistant Principal was close to being at a loss for words.

Most significantly, it was alleged that this event had occurred only forty-five minutes earlier and that the alleged victim had quickly reported the incident to a female teacher in a nearby classroom. My immediate reaction was to think "This is going to be interesting," noting in my mind there was a definite need to determine the truth as quickly as possible due to the possibility of negative media attention. The first thing any school administrator should do when presented with this type of a situation is to sit down and develop a strategic plan for the investigation; knowing it will need to initiated within a short time frame to be most effective.

Putting pen to paper, I wrote down "interview the alleged victim and any identified witnesses, then interview the alleged perpetrator, compare information and take the appropriate action." I first asked my Assistant Principal if he had spoken to anyone about this incident? He commented that he had covertly interviewed the teacher from whose classroom the alleged perpetrator had removed the female student. He stated that she told him that the male teacher asked if he could speak to the ninth grade female about a test she had taken or needed to take. Luckily, this interview was kept under wraps, so I could continue with my investigation without anyone knowing that an official inquiry had been initiated. This does identify one very important point; that being that confidentiality is the key to successfully investigating any incident; the fewer people who know what you are doing, the better.

The alleged victim meekly reported to my office at my request and sat down in a comfortable chair at a conference table located at the other end of the room. One of my female Assistant Principals served as a witness for the interview that would take place. I always recommend having a witness of the same gender present when you are interviewing a student about a matter that could have serious legal implications. Note: Interviewing someone, in particular a possible victim, from behind your desk, where we traditionally sit as school administrators, is a bad idea, so, to improve rapport, speak to them in a more "power neutral position," like at a conference table. I proceeded to calmly ask the young lady to relate the series of events that occurred earlier this day. I did not preempt our conversation with a statement such as "I heard this" or "I heard that" because I did not want to contaminate her testimony, but just let her tell me her version of what transpired. She seemed to be quite credible, not changing her testimony at any time, even when I asked for clarification after she finished.

While she was speaking I was taking down notes, which I advised her, beforehand, I would be doing. Note: don't just start taking notes in the presence of an alleged victim or you will appear too "official," which would not encourage candor on their part. I have often been asked how I could get someone to go into sometimes lurid, personal details with another person present? My answer is quite simple; after you make a quick comment about the other person being there for official purposes and provide the appearance of both sincerity and neutrality, they will turn their attention to you, the person who is asking questions. And, if the situation really gets dicey, that other person may have some personal insight you do not have and may end up asking questions of their own. In most investigative instances, the observer's (e.g. Assistant Principal or School Counselor) primary job is to be present to corroborate statements made, however, I have, on occasion, asked the observer if they had any questions of the person being interviewed.

After the alleged victim finished telling me her story, I went to my computer, wrote up my notes, went over her statement in writing with her and asked her sign it, formalizing her complaint. Within less than one hour, the alleged victim had been interviewed and her written statement had been taken. With no other witnesses identified, I prepared to interview the alleged perpetrator. You will find that the timely reporting of an alleged offense plays a big part in its successful resolution; the sooner the report is made, the more likely it is valid. In this instance, forty-five minutes from commission of the alleged incident to reporting was very timely. No matter what the offense involved is, real victims improve their credibility through timely reporting.

With details of the alleged offense in hand, I asked my Assistant Principal to have the accused male teacher come to my office. When he crossed the threshold of my doorway it was obvious he knew this was about something serious, as did the soldier in the "Lesser of Two Evils" investigation for smuggling hashish in Afghanistan. The first thing I said to him, after I advised him to "please sit down" was "Do you know why I asked you to come to my office?" When he hesitated to answer, I followed up this question with "a ninth grade female student has accused you of kissing, hugging and putting your hand down her pants," followed quickly by "Now if you just kissed and hugged her that is understandable, she is an attractive young lady, but if you put your hand down her pants that would be much more serious and I wouldn't admit that because you'd be in really big trouble!"

While he was pondering the seriousness of my comment I threw in "So tell me, is all you did was kiss and hug her?" Before I could take a breath, out of his mouth came "Yes, all I did was kiss and hug her!" He had made an expected tactical error similar to the one the soldier had made, in this case admitting to a real first "evil" (kissing and hugging the female student) which was, in itself, grounds to terminate him.

What I needed to do was substantiate if he had committed any of the alleged offenses and get him off the school grounds and away from all of my students. It would be up to the police to interview the girl and determine if the male was going to be subject to criminal charges for sexual assault. After he made his admission of misconduct, I informed him that he was suspended. I then called the State Department of Education and informed them he had admitted to engaging in highly inappropriate teacher conduct, at which time they suspended his teaching license.

Again, my immediate goal was not criminal prosecution, but to remove a child predator from my school's environment. If you have played your role professionally, which you surely need to do, an innocent person would never confess to something they didn't do, which means either of the mentioned "evils." In this instance, the timeliness of reporting and the girl's convincing testimony led me to believe she was being truthful. If my internal instinct was not correct, the worst thing that could have happened would have been the receipt of an emphatic "No" on his part, at which time I would have had no choice but to immediately turn the matter over to the police for their investigation. Yes, the police were called for their follow up, right after the teacher confessed to "setting up" the ninth grade girl and kissing and hugging her. I left up the "touching" part of the investigation up to the police. I don't recall hearing about this male teacher ever again.

Case#4
A Case of Sexual Abuse
The Importance of "Listening"

One day one of my Assistant Principals at the elementary level approached me about moving a particular second grade girl to one of the other two classes that served that grade, because the teacher was feeling very uncomfortable as a result of the young lady making comments of a highly sexual nature. I must admit I was rather surprised with what I perceived to be a decided lack of sensitivity on the part of the teacher, who I knew, was herself a mother. Due to the sensitive nature of the matter, I chose to have the female elementary school Assistant Principal interview the young lady in my presence. The conversation that followed between them had one specific purpose, to determine the source that was provoking the comments of a sexual nature; it was not conducted to subvert any DSS or criminal investigation.

As no surprise to me, the second grade girl "knew too much," even taking into consideration the proliferation of information of a sexual nature on television these days. When young lady mentioned her mother's boyfriend "touching her," the interview concluded. What happened next was an immediate call to DSS, which was followed up with an interview of the second grade girl that same day. Next up were local law enforcement, the courts and, eventually, the "boyfriend's" conviction on charges of rape and sexual assault. I was happy to hear the "boyfriend" was sentenced to fifteen years confinement in the state prison. The point I'm attempting to make is again a simple one; "listen" to your children! When a child says something that doesn't make sense in a normal school day context, initiate an investigation and be sure to recognize when you're "over your head" and it's is time to notify the correct investigative authority.

Case Study #5
A Weapon at School?
Sorting Out Truth from Myth

Within the first thirty minutes of my school day, one of my teachers reported to me, in a very emotional manner, that her son, a first grader, had been "robbed at gunpoint in a school stairwell," within the past hour. Her son was a generally well respected student and there was no reason to believe he would lie about such an incident. During his interview, however, which followed shortly thereafter, it appeared there were numerous inconsistencies in his story.

When asked if he knew who, among our small student body (280 students), he could identify as the perpetrator, he remarked that "at first" he could not identify anyone, but that after speaking to a group of fellow student's in the gym after the incident, he could state "he looked like _____." The alleged victim's staff member parent learned about her child's finger-pointing without knowing the context in which his testimony was given (tainted). No, I didn't tell her, as soon as her son's interview was completed she "interviewed him" about what he had told me. She demanded the "identified child" be punished. With all the pressure to successfully resolve this matter, it did not help to have a staff member present in the building who was asking for "blood" because it was her son who was allegedly victimized. Don't forget that the accusation involved a student allegedly wielding a handgun.

As the investigation proceeded that morning, it became quite apparent that no other student had witnessed the event and that the alleged victim's story changed dramatically as he spoke to fellow students about it, to include propositions like "he had a gun, didn't he?," which became part of the student's "story." The staff member continued to put pressure on me to prosecute the student her son had named as the suspect, even though I continually requested that she let the investigation proceed at its own speed.

My next step was not a routine one for me. In an attempt to be as impartial and help the investigation move forward as quickly and effectively as possible, I obtained student yearbook photos and conducted a photo array/line-up for the alleged victim to review. When shown the photographs, which included the one "suggested" by other students in the gym, he was unable to make any identification. In an effort to be thorough, additional interviews were conducted to determine the exact location of the alleged perpetrator that morning. What they revealed was that it would have been physically impossible for him to be at one place in the building and, at the same, at the scene of the alleged offense. Instructional staff, obviously uninvolved adults; were among those providing the alleged perpetrator with an alibi. This was, of course, not good enough for the parent/staff member; nothing would have been. After completing the investigation I came up with the following investigative conclusion: The alleged victim might have been accosted by another student in the hallway; there was no weapon involved, and the victim, a first grader, was not a reliable witness.

Finally, since the parent/ staff member continued to demand "satisfaction," I asked a member of a local law enforcement agency to come to my office to review my investigation. As part of his review, he interviewed the victim and all of my case notes. His conclusion was the same as mine, that "something" happened but we would never know exactly what because the victim's testimony had been manipulated by contact with others. I closed this case involving the alleged use of a weapon to extort money in the files of my office. The parent/staff member was never "friendly" to me again, but I could live with that.

APPENDIX O

Addresses for State and National Charter School Associations

Contacts for National and State Charter School Organizations

National Alliance for Public Charter Schools
1101 15th Street NW, Suite 1010
Washington, DC 20005
Tel: (202) 289-2700 (office)
Fax: (202) 289-4009

Directory of State Charter School Associations
For charter schools in your area, contact your state charter school association.

Alaska Charter Schools Association
Dr. Ginger Blackmon
blackmon_ginger@asdk12.org
258 South Bailey Street
Palmer, AK 99645
Tel: 907.742.1700

Arizona Charter Schools Association
Eileen Sigmund – President

eileen@azcharters.org

azcharters.org

1825 E. Northern Avenue

Phoenix, AZ 85020

Tel: (602) 944-0644

Fax: (602) 680-5743

California Charter Schools Association

Jed Wallace- President & CEO

jed@calcharters.org

www.calcharters.org

250 E 1st St., Suite 1000

Los Angeles, CA 90012

Tel: (213) 244-1446

Fax: (213) 244-144

Colorado League of Charter Schools

Jim Griffin – President

jgriffin@coloradoleague.org

www.coloradoleague.org

725 S. Broadway, Suite 7

Denver, CO 80209

Tel: (303) 989-5356

Fax: (303) 984-9345

Connecticut Charter Schools Network

Jo Lutz – Director

jlutz@ctcharterschoolnetwork.org

http://ctcharterschoolnetwork.org

325 Blue Hills Avenue

Hartford, CT 06112

Tel: (860) 655-6907

Delaware Charter Schools Network
Kendall Massett – Executive Director
kendallm@decharternetwork.org
www.decharternetwork.org/
100 W. 10th St., Suite 1012
Wilmington, DE 19801
Tel: (302) 778-5999

Florida Charter School Alliance
Cheri Shannon – President & CEO
cshannon@flcharteralliance.org
www.flcharteralliance.org/
1900 Biscayne Blvd. Suite 201
Miami, FL 33132
Tel: (954) 881-5467
Florida Consortium of Public Charter Schools
Robert Haag – President of the Board
r.haag@floridacharterschools.org
www.floridacharterschools.org
1126 South Federal Highway Suite 170
Fort Lauderdale, FL 33316
Tel: (850) 222-9595

Georgia Charter Schools Association
Tony Roberts – CEO
troberts@gacharters.org
www.gacharters.org
600 West Peachtree Street, NW, Suite 1555
Atlanta, GA, 30308
Tel: (404) 835-8900
Fax: (888) 799-0837

Hawaii Charter Schools Network
Lynn Finnegan – Executive Director
hcsndirector@gmail.com
www.hawaiicharterschools.com
P.O. Box 3017
Aiea, HI 96701
Tel: (808) 741-5966

Idaho Charter School Network
Diane Demarest – Executive Director
Diane@idahocharterschoolnetwork.com
http://idahocharterschoolnetwork.com
815 W Washington Street, Lower Level Suite
Boise, Idaho 83702
Tel: (208) 906-1420

Illinois Network of Charter Schools
Andrew Broy – President
abroy@incschools.org
www.incschools.org
205 W. Randolph Street, Suite 1340
Chicago, IL 60606
Tel: (312) 629-2063
Fax: (312) 629-2064

Indiana Public Charter Schools Association
Russ Simnick – President
russ@incharters.org
www.incharters.org
407 Fulton Street, Suite 301
Indianapolis, IN 46202
Tel: (317) 972-5880
Fax: (317) 972-5882

Louisiana Association of Public Charter Schools
Caroline Roemer – Executive Director
croemer@lacharterschools.org
http://lacharterschools.org
5500 Prytania Street #126
New Orleans, LA 70115
Tel: (504) 274-3651
Fax: (504) 274-3690

Maine Association for Charter Schools
Roger W. Brainerd, MEd – Executive Director
macs@mainecharterschools.org
mainecharterschools.org
1018 Depot Street
Union, Maine 04862
Tel: 207.785.3071

Maryland Charter School Network
Kimberly Worthington – Executive Director
kworthington@mdcharternetwork.org
www.mdcharternetwork.org
4639 Falls Road
Baltimore, MD 21209
Tel: (800) 689-3795
Fax: (800) 689-3795

Massachusetts Charter Public School Association
Marc Kenen – Executive Director
kenen@masscharterschools.org
www.masscharterschools.org
10 Tremont Street, 6FL
Boston, MA 02108
Tel: (617) 523-0881

Michigan Association of Public School Academies
Dan Quisenberry – President
danquisenberry@charterschools.org
www.charterschools.org
105 W. Allegan, Suite 300
Lansing, MI 48933
Tel: (517) 374-9167
Fax: (517) 374-9197

Minnesota Association of Charter Schools
Eugene Piccolo – Executive Director
eugene@mncharterschools.org
www.mncharterschools.org
161 St Anthony Ave #1000
St Paul, MN 55103
Tel: (651) 789-3090

Missouri Charter Public School Association
Douglas P. Thaman – Executive Director
dthaman@mocharterschools.org
www.mocharterschools.org
3908A Bell Street
Kansas City, MO 64111
Tel: (314) 261-3657

Charter School Association of Nevada
John Hawk- President
jhawk@earlycollegenv.com
www.nevadacharters.org
233 North Stephanie St.
Henderson, NV 89074
Tel: (702) 953-2602
Fax: (702) 953-2609

New Hampshire Public Charter School Association
Eileen Liponis – Director
eileen@liponis.com
www.nhpcsa.org
13 Church Street
Kingston, NH 03848
Tel: (603) 498-2386
Fax: (603) 642-8404

New Jersey Charter Schools Association
Carlos Perez – CEO
cperez@njcharters.org
http://njcharters.org
1 AAA Drive, Suite 201
Hamilton, NJ 08691
Tel: (609) 989-9700
Fax: (609) 989-9745

New Mexico Coalition for Charter Schools
Bruce Hegwer – Executive Director
bruce@nmccs.org
www.nmccs.org
610 Gold Avenue SW, Suite 102
Albuquerque, NM 87102
Tel: (505) 842-8203
Fax: (505) 842-8238

New Mexico Coalition for Charter Schools
Bruce Hegwer – Executive Director
bruce@nmccs.org
www.nmccs.org
610 Gold Avenue SW, Suite 102
Albuquerque, NM 87102

Tel: (505) 842-8203

Fax: (505) 842-8238

New York Charter School Association

Bill Phillips – President

bphillips@nycsa.org

www.nycsa.org

915 Broadway, Suite 110

Albany, NY, 12207

Tel: (518) 694-3110

Fax: (518) 694-3115

Office of Charter Schools

North Carolina Department of Public Instruction

Joel Medley, Director

6303 Mail Service Center

Raleigh, NC 27699-6303

Tel: (919) 807-3491

www.ncpublicschools.org/charterschools

North Carolina Alliance for Public Charter Schools

info@nccharters.org

www.nccharters.org

324 S.Wilmington Street, Suite 405

Raleigh, NC 27601

Tel: (919) 937-2327

www.ncchartersall.org

North Carolina Public Charter Schools Association

Eddie Goodall – Executive Director

eddie@ncpubliccharters.org

http://ncpubliccharters.org

2132 Greenbrook Parkway

Matthews, NC 28104

Tel: (704) 236-1234

Ohio Alliance for Public Charter Schools

Bill Sims – President & CEO

bsims@oapcs.org

www.oapcs.org/

33 N. Third Street Suite 600

Columbus, OH 43215

Tel: (614) 744-2266

Fax: (614) 744-2255

Oklahoma Charter School Association

Steven Huff- Executive Director

stevehuff@cox.net

http://www.okcharters.org

12600 N Kelly Aves

Oklahoma City, OK 73131

Tel: (405) 521-3333

Oregon – The Northwest Center for Educational Options

Karen Heikes – Executive Director

kheikes@nwceo.org

www.nwceo.org/

3439 NE Sandy Blvd # 260

Portland, OR 97232

Tel: (503) 353-1690

Fax: (503) 353-1691

Pennsylvania Coalition of Public Charter Schools

Robert Fayfich – Executive Director

operativ@zbzoom.net

http://pacharters.org/

999 West Chester Pike, Suite B6
West Chester, PA 19382
Tel: (484) 356-0191

The Rhode Island League of Charter Schools
Steve Nardelli – Executive Director
stevenardelli@richarterschools.com
www.richarterschools.com/
4 Richmond Square, Suite 300
Providence, RI 02906
Tel: 401.831.3700 ext. 114
Fax: 401.831.0105

South Carolina Public Charter School District
Dr. Wayne Brazell, Superintendent
3700 Landmark Drive, Suite 201
Columbia, SC 29204
Tel: (803) 734-8322
www.scharters.org

Public Charter School Alliance of South Carolina
Mary Carmichael – Executive Director
Mary.Carmichael@SCCharterSchools.org
www.sccharterschools.org
Physical Address:
140 Stoneridge Drive, Suite 420
Columbia, SC 2921
Tel: (800) 691-7133 ext. 1
Mailing Address:
Public Charter School Alliance of South Carolina
P.O. Box 80444
Charleston, SC 29416

Tennessee Charter School Association
Matt Throckmorton – Executive Director
matt@tncharterschools.org
www.tncharterschools.org
3022 Vanderbilt Place
Nashville, TN 37212
Tel: (615) 339-3349

Texas Charter School Association
David Dunn – Executive Director
ddunn@txcharterschools.org
www.txcharterschools.org
700 Lavaca Street, Suite 930
Austin, Texas 78701
Tel: (512) 584-8272
Fax: (512)584-8492

Utah Association of Public Charter Schools
Chris Bleak – President
chrisrbleak@utahcharters.org
utahcharters.org
PO Box 2583
Salt Lake City, UT 84110
Tel: (801) 960-2583
Fax: (801) 657-4712

Utah Charter Network
Kim Frank -Executive Director
kim@utahcharternetwork.com
utahcharternetwork.com
881 W. State Street
Suite 140-448
Pleasant Grove, UT 84062

Tel: (801) 722-8911

Wisconsin Charter Schools Association
Sarah Granofsky Toce – Executive Director
sgranofsky@wicharterschools.org
www.wicharterschools.org/
P.O. Box 1704
Madison, WI 53701
Tel: (617) 416-7924

Wyoming Association of Public Charter Schools
Kari Cline – Executive Director
kari@wyomingcharters.org
wyomingcharters.org
PO Box 2017
Cheyenne, WY 82003
Tel: (307) 640-6157

APPENDIX P

Letter of Commendation

Date

To

From

Subject: Letter of Commendation

Dear

You are hereby commended for the truly superior job you have performed in the past year in regard to managing our school's testing program. Your flawless performance of duty has significantly contributed to the high esteem in which this school is held by the ..... All of us here at ...... to include the instructional and administrative staff, are indebted to you for ensuring that all testing matters have been, and continue to be, handled in such a highly professional manner.

Thank you again for a job well done!

Sincerely,

Signature Block
Principal
School

APPENDIX Q

Letter of Counseling

Date

Memorandum for Record
From Principal, School
To
Subject: Letter of Counseling

On this date I advised Mr./Ms.................about concerns regarding their use of the term "Shut up!" in the classroom. Mr./Ms. .... advised me that they did say this to a student because they were extremely frustrated. Furthermore, they acknowledged that the use of this phrase with students present was a reflection of poor professionalism on their part.

I further advised them that one particular student was particularly disappointed to hear this from a teacher they had respected before this incident occurred. Mr./Ms. .... offered to exhibit a more caring attitude toward students in the future and I offered him/her the option of sending for me to intervene before they became so frustrated they took it out on the students/children.

Signature Block
Principal
School

APPENDIX R

Letter of Reprimand

....

Date

To

From

Subject: Letter or Reprimand

Mr./Ms:

At about _____, on _____ when you remarked to students and a staff/faculty member present in your classroom that your students were so lazy they were not going to make anything out of themselves in their lives, you let down both your fellow faculty members and members of the school's administrative team. It has been documented you have made this type of highly inappropriate comment on several other occasions, including in the presence of students, parents and staff. When you make negative comments of this nature, it reflects poorly upon all of the school's stakeholders.

Your demonstrated lack of professionalism has seriously injured both your personal and professional reputation. This Letter or Reprimand serves as a final notice that if there is a reoccurrence of this type of highly unprofessional behavior you will be subject to termination of employment at this school.

Signature Block
Principal
School

APPENDIX S

Letter of Admonition

Date

From:

To:

Subject: Letter of Admonition

Mr./Ms:

You are hereby admonished for the unprofessional behavior you exhibited on _____, at which time you left campus with your students under the supervision of an unapproved parent volunteer. The legal implications from your misconduct could have been significant had a student been injured or otherwise compromised in your absence. When you left the campus without first obtaining authority from your academic supervisor and, furthermore, failed to obtain permission for your classroom replacement, you violated numerous school policies and exposed both yourself and this school to serious liability.

This correspondence serves as written notice that you are on a probationary status for the remainder of the school year and that any subsequent violation of school policy may render you subject to termination of employment with this school.

Signature Block
Principal
School

APPENDIX T

Termination of Employment

Date

From

To

Subject: Termination of Employment

Your employment is terminated as of _____.

You have failed to meet expectations for a classroom teacher in several areas, to include ....and failing to effectively put into place recommendations given to you in a Teacher Improvement Plan. The end result of these shortcomings is that your overall teaching performance has been rate as Not Acceptable.

Individuals that provided input toward this decision include _____ and _____. The decision to recommend termination of your employment was unanimous.

Under our school's charter, you have the right to appeal your dismissal to our Board of Directors. Any such request should be put into writing within twenty-four hours so that it may be forwarded by me to them for their review.

Note: Other comments may be placed at this location in the document.

Signature Block
Principal
School

APPENDIX U

Notice of Retention

Date

To the Parents of ....:
Street Address
City
State and Zip Code

After reviewing all available assessments and giving this matter all possible time and thought to come to an alternative conclusion, I am writing to inform you the decision has been made to retain your child, ...in their current grade for the .... school year.

We will all do our very best to help your child catch up academically so they will be fully successful in the years to come.

Sincerely,

Signature Block
School
Principal

APPENDIX V

Bibliography

Deal, Terrence E & Hentsche, Gilbert C. (2004). Adventures of Charter School Creators: Leading from the Ground Up. Scarecrow Education, Lanham, MD.

Light, H. Wayne (2006), Light's Retention Scale, 5th Ed., Academic Therapy Publications, Novato, CA.

O'Hara, Charles C. & O'Hara, Gregory L. (2003). Fundamentals of Criminal Investigation. Charles C. Thomas, LTD, Springfield, IL.

APPENDIX W

Resources

Advanc-ED (School Accreditation)
9115 Westside Parkway
Alpharetta, GA 30009
Tel: (888) 413-3669
www.advanc-ed.org

Blackboard
650 Massachusetts Avenue NW
6th Floor
Washington, DC 20001-3796
Tel: (202) 463-4860
www.blackboard.com

Build With A Purpose (Charter School Construction)
224 Main Street
Metuchen, NJ 08844
(732) 635-1000, ext.153

Carney, Sandoe & Associates
Barry D. Rowland, Senior Search Consultant
44 Blomfield Street
Boston, MA 02108

Tel: (800) 225-7986, (617) 542-0260
Website: www.carneysandoe.com

Center for Educational Reform (Charter School Advocate)
Michelle Tigani
National Offices Tel: (800) 521-2119, (301) 986-8088
Email: cer@edreform.com, www.edreform.com

Charter School Property Solutions (Charter School Construction & Real Estate Development)
2505 Anthem Village Drive
Henderson, NV 89052
Tel: (888) 596-1110
www.csps.us.com

Education Facilities Clearinghouse (High Performing Educational Facilities)
Tel: (800) EFC-0938
Email: askefc@gwu.edu

Great Schools.org (Ratings for Public Schools)

Institute for Effective Schools (Curricular and Testing Protocols)
5901 Sterling Trail
McKinney, TX 75071
Tel: (214) 491-7474

Integrity Real Estate Advisors, Inc. (Charter School Facilities)
Torrey Rush, Director of Advisory Services
500 Lawand Drive, Suite 201
Columbia, SC 29210
Tel: (803) 772-9100
www.IntegrityREA.com

Kelley-Moser Consulting, LLC
150 Harbor Glen Drive
Lexington, SC 29072
Tel: (803) 808-0338
Website: www.kelley-moser.com

Keys to Safer Schools (School Safety)
Mike Nelson, Director
P.O. Box 296, Bryant, AR 72023-0298. Tel: (800) 504-7355
www.keystosaferschools.com

Legal Notes for Education
Tel: (800)220-5000
www.legalnotesforeducation.com

National Alliance for Public Charter Schools
1101 15th Street NW, Suite 1010
Washington, DC 29005
Tel: (202) 289-2700

National Charter School Resource Center
Website: http://charterschoolcenter.org/priority-area/facilities-financing

National Resource Center on Charter School Finance and Governance

Preferred Meals (Charter School USDA-approved lunch program)
Corporate Offices
5240 St. Chares Road, Berkeley, IL 60163
Tel: (800) 886-6325
www.preferredmeals.com

Self-Help Credit Union (Charter School Financing)
301 West Main Street

Durham, NC 27701
Website: www.self-help.org

Smithson Inc. (Charter School Construction)
Jim Carson
1661 Wesleyan Blvd.
Rocky Mount, NC 27802
Email: jimmie@smithsonnet.com
Tel: (252) 977-3055

Vanguard Modular (Charter School Construction)
Steve Earnhardt
115 Crasby Avenue, Lowell, NC 29098
Tel: 1(877) 438-8627
Email: searnhardt@vanguardmodular.com
Website: www.vanguardmodular.com

APPENDIX X

Consulting w/Dr. von Rohr

Dr. von Rohr is available for consulting to assist you in either starting up or successfully operating your charter school, in any of the areas covered in this book. He may be reached via email at jmvonrohr@aol.com or by telephone at (864) 764-4722. If you need assistance, please contact him.

Printed in the United States
By Bookmasters